# The Homebrewed Christianity
# Guide to the Holy Spirit

# The Homebrewed Christianity Guide to the Holy Spirit

## Hand-Raisers, Han, and the Holy Ghost

**GRACE JI-SUN KIM**
AUTHOR

**TRIPP FULLER**
SERIES EDITOR

Fortress Press
Minneapolis

THE HOMEBREWED CHRISTIANITY GUIDE TO
THE HOLY SPIRIT
Hand-Raisers, Han, and the Holy Ghost

Copyright © 2018 Fortress Press. All rights reserved. Except
for brief quotations in critical articles or reviews, no part
of this book may be reproduced in any manner without
prior written permission from the publisher. Email copy-
right@1517.media or write to Permissions, Fortress Press,
PO Box 1209, Minneapolis, MN 55440-1209.

Cover design: Jesse Turri
Book design: PerfecType, Nashville, TN

Print ISBN: 978-1-4514-9956-8
eBook ISBN: 978-1-5064-0124-9

The paper used in this publication meets the minimum
requirements of American National Standard for Informa-
tion Sciences — Permanence of Paper for Printed Library
Materials, ANSI Z329.48-1984.

Manufactured in the U.S.A.

To my firstborn son, Theodore Andrew Ho-Jun Lee,
on the occasion of his twentieth birthday,
who has been a constant inspiration for my life.

# Contents

# Series Introduction

You are about to read a guidebook. Not only is the book the sweet "guidebook" size, shaped perfectly to take a ride in your back pocket, but the book itself was crafted with care by a real-deal theology nerd. Here's the thing. The Homebrewed Christianity Guide series has one real goal: we want to think *with* you, not *for* you.

The whole "homebrew" metaphor grows from my passion for helping anyone who wants to geek out about theology to do so with the best ingredients around. That's why I started the Homebrewed Christianity podcast in 2008, and that's why I am thrilled to partner with Fortress Press's Theology for the People team to produce this series. I am confident that the church has plenty of intelligent and passionate people who want a more robust conversation about their faith.

A podcast, in case you're wondering, is like talk radio on demand without the commercials. You download a file and listen when, if, where, and how long you want. I love the podcast medium. Short of talking one-on-one, there's hardly a more intimate presence than speaking to someone in their earbuds as they're stuck in traffic, on the treadmill, or washing dishes. When I started the podcast,

I wanted to give anyone the option of listening to some of the best thinkers from the church and the academy.

Originally, the podcast was for friends, family, and my local pub theology group. I figured people in the group were more likely to listen to a podcast than read a giant book. So as the resident theology nerd, I read the books and then interviewed the authors. Soon, thousands of people were listening. Since then the audience has grown to over fifty thousand unique listeners each month and over a million downloads. A community of listeners, whom we call Deacons, grew, and we've got a cast of cohosts and regular guests.

Over the better part of a decade, I have talked to scores of theologians and engaged with the Deacons about these conversations. It has been a real joy. Every time I hear from a listener, I do the happy dance in my soul.

And here's the deal: I love theology, but I love the church more. I am convinced that the church can really make a difference in the world. But in order to do that, it needs to face reality rather than run from it. The church must use its brain, live its faith, and join God in working for the salvation of the world. And that's what these books are all about.

We often open and close the podcast by reminding listeners that we are providing the ingredients so that they can brew their own faith. That's the same with these books. Each author is an expert theological brewer, and they've been asked to write from their own point of view. These guidebooks are not boringly neutral; instead, they are zestily provocative, meant to get you thinking and brewing.

I look forward to hearing from you on the Speakpipe at HomebrewedChristianity.com and meeting you at an HBC 3D event. We can drink a pint and talk about this book, how you agree and disagree with it. Because if we're talking about theology, the world is a better place.

And remember: Share the Brew!

Tripp Fuller

# The Homebrewed Posse

Whether it's the podcast, the blog, or live events, Homebrewed Christianity has always been a conversation, and these books are no different. So inside of this and every volume in the HBC book series, you'll be hearing from four members of the Homebrewed community. They are:

**THE BISHOP**

**The Bishop:** Kindly, pastoral, encouraging. She's been around the block a few times, and nothing ruffles her feathers. She wants everyone to succeed, and she's an optimist, so she knows they will.

**THE ELDER**

**The Elder:** Scolding, arrogant, know-it-all. He's old and disgruntled, the father figure you can never please. He loves quoting doctrine; he's the kind of guy who controls every church meeting because he knows Roberts Rules of Order better than anyone else.

## THE DEACON

**The Deacon:** Earnest, excited, energetic. He's a guy who has just discovered HBC, and he can't get enough of it. He's a cheerleader, a shouter, an encourager. He's still in his first naïveté.

## THE ACOLYTE

**The Acolyte:** Smart, inquisitive, skeptical. She's the smartest student in your confirmation class. She's bound to be a biologist or a physicist, and she's skeptical of all the hocus pocus of Christianity. But she hasn't given up on it yet, so her questions come from the heart. She really wants to know if all this stuff works.

We look forward to continuing the conversation with you, online and in person!

# Introduction

When I first sat down with Tripp Fuller and Tony Jones to discuss writing for the Homebrewed Christianity (HBC) series, it was over beers. No surprise there. What maybe did surprise them was that I insisted on writing the volume on the Holy Spirit. That's because I think the church has no future unless the Spirit is at the center. For real. The church is going to be as relevant as the members of *NSYNC not named Justin if it doesn't get full of the Holy Ghost.

Don't worry, I am not about to lay hands on you through these pages, causing you to fall down and speak in tongues. I am Presbyterian, after all. What I am going to tell you is something that might get you frustrated or excited—or hopefully both. The Father and the Son get way too much play. For two millennia, the church has talked nonstop about the Father and Son and has treated the Spirit like bicycle training wheels: you keep the Spirit around to lean on when the two Dudes run into a problem, but otherwise you ignore it.

I'll try to say this charitably. According to Saint Augustine, the Father and the Son *require* the Spirit. The

**THE ACOLYTE**

If tongues aren't required and we get a little less "dude," I'm ready to get Spirit filled.

Spirit is the bond of love that sustains their relationship in the heart of God. I am simply updating that to say the church needs the Spirit just as much. Here are four reasons (because three would be too obvious):

Ignoring the presence and activity of the Spirit leaves Christians thinking like deists, where God is up and out while we are down and in the world. We're alone, unless and until the Son interrupts, as he occasionally does, for one of his big arrivals.

Not surprisingly, when God talk is 90 percent about Father and Son, there are material consequences—for example, the relegation of women, the planet, and non-Christian neighbors to the sidelines. You might not think these are connected, but I will show you the connection and introduce you to someone who completely disagrees with me in the most legit way.

Nota bene, the entire Hebrew Bible is obsessed with the Spirit, Jesus talks about it nonstop, and so does Paul. I am just saying, as a *biblical* feminist theologian, that the Spirit should be at the center of our faith. Too often, our conservative Christian friends replaced the Spirit in the Trinity with the Bible and only focused on the Bible to the detriment of the Spirit. Our progressive Christian friends just stopped reading the Bible and have thus also forgotten the Spirit.

Paying attention to the Spirit is especially relevant in today's context. Today's church and the spiritual ecosystem in which it operates are more diverse and global than they ever have been. Might it make sense to focus on the very theological doctrine that insists God is actually present and a part of this diversity? Maybe, if we learn to listen to the Spirit through them, we can even be blessed and not threatened by this reality.

## Theological Purity Kills

For too long, theology has been done by white European men. Other global voices around the world have not been taken into consideration, as the old-boys' club felt that they may bring impurity to theology. What white European men did was usually viewed as pure and real theology, and most things outside of that tight-knit circle were viewed as "unorthodox." It was believed that outside thoughts would contaminate theology. However, if we listen only to the old-boys' club, we will never understand the magnitude, depth, and beauty of God.

Theological purity kills. We need to hear global voices, especially from the margins, which will add depth to our understanding of God. Different cultures, histories, and experiences can help us walk toward a more freeing understanding of God as Spirit whose presence can be felt all around the world.

The Spirit God is infinite, and we are finite beings. Our experiences and contexts limit our understanding of the one who created us. We need to recognize that theology is affected by cultures, other religions, customs, and practices. For example, Christians around the world observe Easter and consider it one of the holiest events in the Christian calendar. However, many of the practices around Easter are rooted in ancient pagan practices related to the spring equinox. The sooner we acknowledge this, the faster we will reconcile ourselves to the understanding that theology was never pure. Recognizing this will give birth to a theology that challenges the status quo, destroys inequity, and promotes justice and liberation.

## Spirit-Filled Syncretism

Different cultures, religions, and ideas clash. But when they clash, new ideas and forms emerge, offering beautiful new ways to view the world, religion, and God. The Spirit moves and hovers over the earth. It blows like the wind, and thus we cannot predict which way it will move. We feel the results of the movement, but we cannot predict it, and we definitely cannot control it.

The Spirit is vibrant and alive. As it moves, we come to understand it not as pure but as a movement that is syncretistic and holy. Globally, different people have different words that evoke the Spirit. Though the words may not all be the same, these words express a similar concept. The Israelites called it *ruach*, the New Testament church called it *pneuma*, German theologians called it *geist*, and Asian theologians call it *Chi*. These different words have similar meanings but also show a syncretistic view of the Spirit. How Asians experience the everyday movement and power of the Spirit may not be the same as how South Americans will experience the Spirit. But the various ways we experience, understand, and talk about the Spirit all add richness.

Anyone else having flashbacks to apologetics training on syncretism? So much fear of the Other.

**THE ELDER**

We recognize that the Spirit isn't dead, as some Eurocentric theology has portrayed, but rather, it is alive and affecting the world. The world experiences this in so many ways, and these experiences are a testament to the beauty, power, and wonder of the Spirit, who continues to stir us to work for justice.

# Creation Vibrates

It is genuinely difficult to talk about the Spirit, and I should know. I grew up in a church so Jesus centered that I don't really recall a time when the Spirit was preached or talked. I think that's because talking about the Spirit feels vague and intangible. For most of my life, I didn't want to study it or even talk about it. In my master of divinity studies, I avoided taking any classes on the Holy Spirit, and I managed to do the same in my PhD program. I then avoided dealing with the question for the next decade. Only recently did I feel the desire to begin reading about it.

My avoidance of the Spirit is typical of many theologians. I sympathize with readers who feel the Holy Spirit is difficult to understand. But that's no excuse, so let's dive in!

Modernity has flattened our understanding of the world and given us reductive modes of inquiry. This has had consequences in how we think about the world and about God, leaving no room for a dynamic, present view of the world and God's presence in it. Many of us do not feel permission to view a moving and vibrant Spirit. If we continue to live in a world where God is contestable and mechanistic accounts of the world reign, the Spirit can easily be neglected. What this means is that the church and "secular logic" ignore and relegate the Spirit. As we look in a new direction to see how the Spirit participates in our vibrant world, we want to trek back through the Bible and see how the Spirit changed the lives of the Israelites.

## The Holy Spirit in the Old Testament

Our Christian understanding of the Holy Spirit comes from the Bible, the church, and our own experiences. Many who have ignored the Holy Spirit will be pleasantly surprised that the Spirit was vibrant, alive, and moving among the Israelites during the Old Testament period. In the original Hebrew, the word *ruach* appears 405 times in the books of the Old Testament, used in various forms to mean the Spirit of God, the spirit of humanity, and good and evil spirits, as well as wind, breath, soul, life-giving spirit, and God. Many biblical narratives unveil the power and splendor of the Spirit. For example, the first verses of Genesis employ the feminine noun *ruach* to speak of the mothering, life-giving Spirit of God that hovered and brooded over the deep at creation.

I am pretty sure *ruach* is the most popular Hebrew word in the tattoo parlor.

**THE ACOLYTE**

Wind is often linked to *ruach*. One cannot see the wind, just as one cannot see the Spirit. But as one can see the effects of the wind, one can also see the effects of the Spirit. Wind was understood to be caused by God.

I once was part of a group of Korean-American Presbyterian ministers who traveled to Hawaii as part of a pastoral consultation to visit some churches, including several Methodist congregations, and see how they emerged and sustained themselves over the years. One afternoon, a United Methodist district superintendent gave a presentation with a wonderful history of the church in Hawaii. He explained why there were so many Methodist churches in Hawaii and fewer Presbyterian ones: when the two denominations were deciding on which areas to evangelize, the Methodists decided to go to Hawaii, and the Presbyterians to Alaska, which led one of us to joke, "That gives a new meaning to the 'frozen chosen'!"

The ones into total depravity picked Alaska. Not surprised.

**THE ELDER**

Presbyterians like me are often afraid to live out the Pentecostal vision. Presbyterians like to do things "decently and in order," which means that it is rare to see Presbyterians as "Spirit-filled" Christians. We are reserved churchgoers and don't necessarily want to raise hands and allow the Holy Spirit to come upon us. Like the Israelites, we may feel that we are the chosen, but we do not want to publicly live the Pentecostal life.

However, occasionally, the Presbyterian church that I attend will invite a guest preacher with some Pentecostal tendencies. I remember one who was preaching up in the pulpit, and in the middle of his long sermon, he started saying "Amen!" He expected the people sitting in the pews to respond to his *Amen*, but that never happened. He continued repeating the word. He paced back and forth near the pulpit, raised his arms in the air, and even shouted parts of his sermon. Occasionally, you heard a faint *Amen* from the pews. But generally, it was a "frozen chosen" crowd.

The Israelites were the chosen people, and God was with them. They felt the power of the Spirit as they were fleeing Egypt and came to the Red Sea. The Spirit as wind was real to them. The power of the Spirit as wind was upon the sea as Moses called upon God to save them. The Spirit came as a gusty wind and spread the sea apart. The root of the word *ruach* was probably an onomatopoetic word for a gale, the strong wind—*ruach*—that divided the Red Sea for Israel's exodus from Egypt (Exodus 14:21).[1] As an onomatopoetic word, it imitated the "whoosh" or blowing sound made by a strong wind. This force was seen as the power of the almighty God.

The Hebrew people migrated to Egypt during a time of famine. After many generations, a new Egyptian ruler who came to power enslaved the Hebrews. At first, the suffering slaves could find no way to freedom. But God called Moses to deliver the Hebrew people out of Egypt.

Initially, Moses was reluctant to obey. He is much like us, resistant to God's call and God's work. The work looks difficult, costly (even health and life threatening), disturbing, and at odds with our own intentions. But eventually, Moses did respond to the call and mustered the courage to demand that Pharaoh let the people go. When Pharaoh refused, God sent plagues upon the Egyptians. After ten horrible plagues, Pharaoh gave in and let the Israelites go free.

As the Hebrew people came to the Red Sea on their way out of Egypt, they were horrified to find that Pharaoh had a change of heart and sent his army of war chariots after them. As the people stood before the Red Sea with the Egyptians bearing down behind them, Moses lifted his staff in the air, and the Red Sea parted with the help of "a strong east wind all night [that] made the sea dry land," (Exodus 14:21) so they could escape Pharaoh's chariot. They stood in wonder and delight in the power of the wind. They experienced liberation, hope, and mercy through the wind that parted the sea and gave them a walk toward freedom.

---

I pray for the day I hear this story and *do not* think of Charlton Heston.

**THE BISHOP**

The image of the Holy Spirit as redemptive power is perhaps best seen in this account of the Exodus from Egypt. People can recognize the actions of God by their effect on the people and the world. These manifestations of the Holy Spirit of God were both practical and encouraging for the Hebrew people, affirming for them that God was present and would continue to work in their lives. It assured them that God would not abandon them.

However, although the Hebrews recognized God in the wind, they experienced their own difficulties. After their escape, their forty years in the desert taught them the destructive side of the wind.

## Walking in the Desert

If you have ever walked in a desert, you know the harm that wind and sand can have. There are several forms of desert. Some are primarily sand, such as the Sahara Desert, which is the largest hot desert, with large sand dunes and long stretches of sand between oases. There are also rocky deserts with cacti and other thorny bushes that can survive in the dry heat.

A few years ago, I took several seminary and college students to Nogales, Mexico, with the BorderLinks program to study immigration and the plight of Mexicans crossing the desert into the United States.[2] BorderLinks took us on a short walk in the desert to get a firsthand experience of its difficulties and hardships. They warned us to wear long pants, as there are flying cacti (jumping cholla) and thorny bushes that will cling to your legs and cause lacerations. Of course, students never listen to instructions. Several students wore shorts, thinking they would be safe.

---

I am confident that knowledge of "flying cacti" would have an impact on my wardrobe.

**THE ACOLYTE**

---

Within five minutes of walking through the desert, several students were yelling for help. The flying cacti had attached themselves to the students' legs. It was quite a sight as the students tried to pull the thorny cacti off their legs. With some help from the BorderLinks staff, my students were freed from the cacti. The BorderLinks leader explained that when the US Border Patrol flew around in the desert, looking for migrant workers coming into the United States, they would hover their helicopters low, causing the sand to swirl into their eyes, and cacti, loose branches, and thorns would fly around as well. This tactic was used to discourage entry into the United States, demonstrating the destructive power of the wind and its effects on the migrants.

The Hebrew people had a similar experience as they wandered in the desert for forty years. They recognized the power of the Spirit of God as wind, but they also feared it. Either way, the wind was a power that blew as it wished, and no human had the ability to tell which way it would blow.

It is through these earliest connections with the natural world that the Hebrew people experienced God. The Spirit of God who breathes liberation into the world does not abandon the people but continues to lead them and sustain them. In the wind, fire, and provision of food such as manna during the exodus journey, we see powerful symbols for the Spirit of God. That Spirit guided the people as a pillar of cloud in the day and a pillar of fire by night (Exodus 14:19, 20). We who live in the modern world with technology, computers, and the internet lose touch with the natural world and turn our attention instead to smart phones packed with entertainment, connections, messages, and whatever else we believe we need to function.

## Child's Play

Parents recognize that children spend more time inside playing with video games, television, computers, or other technical gadgets than the generations before them, who spent time outside, running on the grass, climbing trees, or making up games in the natural world. We have forgotten that we owe creation to God. The understanding of the Holy Spirit as wind brings us back to a primordial, earthly reality. We need to get back in touch with nature and recognize the Holy Spirit as the wind in everything and everywhere.

With our detachment from nature, many of us have made the Holy Spirit into an intellectual exercise. Instead of seeing the Holy Spirit alive and participating in our world, we have made it a mere philosophical concept, not an embodied one. We forget that it is alive, moving, and

Does this mean that when I blew into my old Nintendo cartridges, I was putting the Holy Spirit into my *Mario Bros.* and *Duck Hunt* games?

**THE DEACON**

around us. We forget that the wind of the Holy Spirit is with us and within us as we move through our lives. The wind blows where it wishes, and we need to recognize in it the power of God's presence. We need a reminder that God the Spirit is present and in our midst. Just as the Israelites witnessed the power of the Holy Spirit as the wind parting the Red Sea, we need to recognize its power in our own daily lives. God's presence is so often neglected and hidden from our lives. The Spirit of God lives among us, and we need to acknowledge it.

I remember some of my elementary-school teachers, like the young Mrs. Kaufman, my beloved second-grade teacher. She had long, flowing black hair, parted in the middle, that reached the lower part of her back. Students in grades two and three would line up after school to give her a hug and kiss and say their good-byes. Looking back, this seems totally insane. Why would a bunch of kids line up after school to give her a kiss and a hug? But we did it every day as we all walked to and from school. The students all wanted to show their love to a beautiful teacher.

One other teacher who stands out in my memory is my third-grade teacher, Mrs. Schwartz. She had black cropped hair with a few gray strands. She loved to wear a nice top with dark black slacks. She was dearly loved by all her students, and the students felt like she was their grandmother. She always had a loving and gentle smile on her face. She was also the school choir conductor, and her love for music was evident in all that she did.

Mrs. Schwartz was a Christian and belonged to the old Presbyterian church in downtown London, Ontario. She had a special affection for the Korean immigrant students at my school. She invited me and two other Korean girls to perform a dance and song at her church. We practiced the short dance and song for months. We were to wear our traditional Korean dresses, *ham-bok,* which are made of colorful silk and usually decorated with embroidered flowers or designs. I really loved wearing my *ham-bok*, as it made me look like a little Korean princess.

We practiced for months, and I was nervous the night of the performance at the Presbyterian church. We sat beside Mrs. Schwartz in the front pew in front of the large organ pipes, which can be found in many Presbyterian churches. I was so nervous that I ended up wetting my pants in the church pew, waiting for my turn to perform. It was the most embarrassing night of my life, as I was dressed like a princess and was supposed to perform like a rock star. As I felt the warmness moving along the pew, I did my best to cover it up with my silk Korean dress. But I could not cover up the urine smell. I was totally mortified, but Mrs. Schwartz just pretended that nothing had happened. That was pure grace in an awful situation.

Mrs. Schwartz was known for her kindness and sweetness. She had an uncanny ability to get students to enjoy and love music. She always carried a small black

Is anyone else thinking of the scene in *Big Daddy* where Adam Sandler's character pees his pants to save the kid from embarrassment?

**THE ACOLYTE**

pitch pipe in her pocket, which she used for various purposes in the classroom. She would blow a note to get the class attention. If the students didn't quiet down, she would blow it again and again until we were all settled and at attention. She also used the pitch pipe when she directed the primary class choir. Before we ever sang a note, she would gently put the pitch pipe on her thin, pursed lips and blow into it, giving us the right pitch to begin our song. After blowing in the pitch pipe, she'd then hum the note, raise her arms, and begin to conduct the choir.

This pitch pipe became synonymous with Mrs. Schwartz. She valued music, and the vibration that she found in the pitch pipe always brought some sense of control in the classroom. That clear pitch prepared us to begin singing a song and gave us a sense of vibration and music as part of life.

Vibrations occurred when Mrs. Schwartz blew the pitch pipe and hummed the note. Vibrations occurred as we sang the beautiful songs in our choir. I learned early that vibrations fill our lives, and vibrations make this world a beautiful and enchanting place. Vibrations happen in all aspects of our lives.

Vibrations are part of God's creation. The Spirit is vibration and hovers over the earth. All things vibrate and are formed by vibration.

## Creation Vibrates

If all things vibrate and vibrations are part of this world, then were all things created by God through acts of vibration? This is an important question to ask as we explore beyond the Eurocentric and patriarchal models of understanding the Holy Spirit. Science and religion have much to say to each other concerning many of the problems we face. As we try to understand the Spirit, it is time to revisit Pythagoras's ideas on "the music of the spheres." Philosophy offers clues to why things vibrate.

The notion of vibration as a creative force is very old, dating back at least to Pythagoras and Plato's dialogue *Timaeus*. After Timaeus has given a prelude to his principal speech about the nature of creation, Socrates instructs him to "do for us what comes next in order and perform the song (*nomos*) itself."[3] Plato, carrying on a tradition begun by Pythagoras, associated the workings of the universe with vibrations, which are the basis of music. Timaeus characterizes the state of things before creation—that which is chaotic and without order—as being unmusical. What *is* intelligible is musical. The creator made it impossible for the intellect to exist in anything except the soul; then by placing the soul within the body, the creator joined together all that was beautiful and intelligible in our bodies.

Even before Plato, Pythagoras discovered the relations between vibrations and music.[4] Many ancient mystery religions were based on arcane symbols, secret rites and ceremonies, and most importantly, music. The pure tones of musical instruments were considered closest to the divine. And how are these tones produced? By vibrations, of course, as sound waves are produced by high and low pressures in the air, whereby sounds are sensed by the ear.[5] Pythagoras discovered a remarkable number of characteristics of musical vibrations through his observations of the differences in tone produced by plucking strings drawn traut with various weights. That same effect is recreated every day with all types of stringed instruments, from guitar to piano, when the tone produced by plucking a string is determined by the tension on the string, created by the tuning posts.

The creation story talks about the *ruach Elohim* (wind/breath of God), which "vibrated" over the chaos (Genesis 1:2). God creates everything through the word, speaking in the creative energies of the *ruach*. All creatures come to life through the same *ruach*, and it is this that constitutes the community of creation. All creatures are given life through the vibrating breath of God.

God, who hovers over the earth, allows the vibrations to fill us and move us. In the Genesis creation story, the Spirit vibrates and gives birth to new things. In the beginning, the raging ocean covers everything, and all is in total darkness. Out of this darkness, the Spirit of God moves over the water (Genesis 1:2) and creates heaven and earth in six days. Whatever God commands or speaks is created. "Let there be light!" and light appears (Genesis 1:3). Through the vibration of this command, God creates the world. As the days of creation pass, the vibration image intensifies. God speaks and then can cocreate with creation. God says, "Let the water be filled" (Genesis 1:20), and then God also says, "Let the ground bring forth" (Genesis 1:24).

**THE BISHOP**

Imagining the link between vibrations and voice can help us remember the power of voice.

The creation account in Genesis 1 reminds us that God has magnificently created this world. We must remain mindful of this and not destroy what God has created by our greediness, for everything that God created is good. Further, the life of all things and the breath of all people are in the hands of the Spirit. Job 12:10 states, "In his hand is the life of every living thing and the breath of every human being."

**THE ELDER**

One reason I flinch at so much Spirit talk is that it reminds me of my dependence on God, others, and a creation I can't control.

God's words vibrate and creation comes into being. In Luke 21:33, Jesus says, "Heaven and earth will pass away, but my words will never pass away." We recognize the infinite in these words. If God's words last forever and we recognize God as the infinite, we come to understand that God and the Word are same (John 1). God as Word is vibration that sets creation in motion and is part of the ongoing creation today.

Creation lives through the presence of the divine Spirit. The energies of God's own Spirit bring forth creation, and God constantly strengthens creation through the gift of *ruach*. Life depends on breath. God breathes the breath of life and sustains our life. It is the Spirit that bridges the gap between Creator and creature.

Created in God's image, the human creature also creates, thus participating in divine creativity. Human creativity is not itself divine, but it brings the human creature into the sphere of the Spirit's power. If humanity can recognize that God is in all things, we will develop a stronger incentive to take care of the earth and all that is in it. This understanding must inspire us to reverent care for the earth. We are commanded to do no less.

Creation is not static. It is full of movement and vibration. The vibration of all living things reminds us of the Spirit's creative, life-breathing work: "When you send your Spirit, they are created and you renew the face of the earth" (Psalm 104:30). Vibrations allow us to expand the word *creation* to include cocreation, even coining a new word, *creationing*. The generative relationship of God's investment in the world includes vibration and relational movement.

**THE DEACON**

I like "creationing." It beats "cocreator," which reminds me of group projects in school, where you get extra work and no legit help.

All this creationing and vibrating make us a kind of creative orchestra that we witness and participate in every day. In so doing, we experience God's love. We need to allow the movement of God's Spirit as vibration to move in our lives. We need to allow the creative power of the Spirit to vibrate through us, move us, and make us move.

When we instead become more anthropocentric and self-centered, we fail to see the redemptive love that waits to be recognized in everything. If we can begin to open ourselves to the expectation that others also hold wisdom and truth about God, we can work toward a new harmony: a new heaven and a new earth that we can reach through the vibration of the Spirit.

## Breathe In, Breathe Out

Breathing is essential to life. It keeps us alive; it sustains life; it is an essential sign of life, as natural as life itself. After I gave birth to each of my three children, the first thing that came out of my mouth was "Are they breathing?" After a difficult pregnancy and a long painful delivery, all you want to know is whether your baby is breathing. Nothing is more essential.

Breath evokes the sense of the intimacy and presence of the Spirit, who is with us always, even when we are unaware of it. *Ruach* is the breath of life and the power to live (Ecclesiastes 12:7). In the Old Testament, life-sustaining breath comes directly from the Divine—the creative power of Yahweh, who bestowed life upon creation (Job 27:3).

We see God's sustaining creation through *ruach* clearly in the book of Job, often thought to be the oldest book in the Bible. It expresses the ways in which the life of all things and the breath of all people are in the hands of the Spirit (Job 12:10), and death comes when God withdraws God's Spirit (Job 34:13–15).[6] Through the Holy Spirit, God created the world and breathed life into it. God is the one who breathes the breath of life into empty shells and brings them to life. The breath of God creates and sustains.

In Genesis 2:7, it is after God breathes into Adam that Adam comes alive. The word used in the text to refer to God's breath is *neshama*, which is a synonym of *ruach*. *Ruach* is used to mean "breath of life," as in Ezekiel 37, when the dry bones in the valley come to life as a result of God's *ruach*.

Creation emerges out of the energies of God's own Spirit, bridging the gulf between Creator and creature, actor and act, and master and work. Human creativity is intimately bound up in God's own creativity. *Ruach* can give life to the lifeless and bring renewed life to those who have no hope. The Spirit of God is at work in creation.

The creativity of God begins in creation itself: the creative act of God that brings all things into existence and coexistence. "This breath is the essence of life" (Job 12:10), and without it is death. And all life is derived from one

**THE ACOLYTE**

I like the idea of God's Spirit being at work in creation, but all too often, it doesn't feel right.

source, which is God. Thus, life and death are dependent upon the presence of the divine breath, as in Job 34:14: "If he should take back his spirit to himself, and gather to himself his breath." God's *ruach* sustains the being of the universe and energizes its processes. God is constantly present and breathes with the breath of the world.

Breath is a vital element of all living beings. In Genesis 2, God formed man from the dust of the ground, breathed into his nostrils the breath (*neshama*) of life, and gave life to this human. Later, when the divine Spirit disappears from the living creature, only dust will be left: "for you are dust, and to dust you shall return" (Genesis 3:19).

**THE BISHOP**

Having been honored to sit with many dear people as they breathed their last, I understand how powerful this image is.

*Ruach* and the biblical concept of *ruach Elohim* (the breath of God) portray God as life giving; *ruach* alone denotes the life force of the individual. Only God gives and protects the life force: the ultimate source of life and the one who sustains life. The Spirit of God is recognized at the beginning of the Bible as it plays its role in the creation story. The Holy Spirit as breath is the force that gives life to all life in the cosmos (Genesis 1:2). As it does so, creation becomes understood as an act of God. The Holy Spirit moves the biosphere and gives life to everything in it.

## Prophetic Power

The Spirit is the basis for a prophetic ministry. This is about God's pronouncement of God's presence on this earth. It is about moving forward to help those in need. It is about shaking people up to recognize the power of God, as when Ezekiel experiences a vision of a field full of dried-up human bones and hears God's call to prophesy: "So, I prophesied as I had been commanded; . . . I looked, and there were sinews on them, and flesh had come upon them, and skin had covered them; but there was no breath in them. . . . I prophesied as he commanded me, and the breath came into them, and they lived, and stood on their feet, a vast multitude" (Ezekiel 37:7–10). The prophetic power of the Spirit gave life in Ezekiel, and it is the promise also given to us that we also will receive life.

This passage gives hope to those whose life seems to be laid out like "them dry bones," with hopelessness and little will to live. In the depths of despair, we are given hope that we can turn to God, who is the powerful life-giving Spirit that can give power, strength, and love to those who come before God. God can give life even to dry bones.

Skin covered up the dry bones, and then the breath of God came upon them and gave them life. I was introduced to this story as a kid in Sunday school. The horror of bones coming to life threw me off, and I had nightmares after hearing it. Now that I'm older, I recognize the beauty rather than the horror of bones coming to life—that Ezekiel is a Hebrew prophet who prophesies about the destruction of Jerusalem, the restoration to the land of Israel, and the Third Temple. We need to see the dry bones in terms of the prophetic tradition that allowed the Spirit to come into the Israelite's lives to work and give them life.

**THE DEACON**

I had some seriously bad dreams when I realized God had drowned all but two puppies in the flood. Some Bible stories are not meant for children's bedtime.

The Old Testament shows the Spirit—not just any spirit, but a life-giving Spirit of God—as the divine power that creates, sustains, and renews life (Genesis 1:2). This power of the Spirit is found in the prophetic books of Isaiah, Ezekiel, and Joel. For God to bring breath to dry bones shows the power of the Spirit to give life, always. Even in situations of death, sorrow, despair, and hopelessness, the Spirit can move us and create a space of joy to be alive. If it can bring back to life what was dead, what more can the Spirit do for us?!

Just as there was power in the wind that the Israelites experienced in the desert and in the Red Sea, there also is power in the valley of the dry bones. The Spirit of God moves, strengthens us, and gives full life. God as Spirit is the source of life and sustains life. In Psalm 36:9, God is called the well of life.

The creative power of God is the transcendent face of *ruach*. Its immanent side is the power to live, which is enjoyed by everything that is alive. God's *ruach* is present when God wills it to be, present in everything and life sustaining.

Spirit has a vitally important relation to the prophets. The Spirit came down upon the people, and the prophets proclaimed their understanding of it. When the Israelites walked through the Red Sea and emerged safely on the other side, the Spirit overcame the prophet Miriam, Moses's sister, in her hymn of praise. The Spirit interacts with our inner lives—not only our inner selves, but the world in which we find ourselves.

The world of the Israelites in Egypt was bound up in slavery. It was unacceptable. Not only did slavery value one group of people over another, it denied the liberty of a whole people, treating them as less than human. Slavery, though unjust in the extreme, still exists in contemporary human trafficking. People are treated as commodities all over the world, either for manual labor or in the sex industry. This abominable situation, which we are allowing to continue, must be addressed and changed. The Spirit of God is concerned not only about the condition of our inner beings but also about the degrading conditions that peoples must endure throughout the world.

We must allow the Spirit to come in and move us, as it moved Miriam to prophesy. The first prophetess who sang a song after the exodus, she becomes a paradigm of the prophetic spirit. She watched over Moses as he lay in a basket in the river; she made sure that a member of Pharaoh's family would pull him from the river. She becomes an embodiment of celebration as she tells the princess that she will find a woman to raise the baby and bring him back to the palace as a child. She becomes an embodiment of the Spirit as she sings and celebrates the exodus. The Spirit is present in the lives of the Israelites. The Spirit is providential.

**THE ACOLYTE**

I didn't realize how much there is to Miriam's story.

## God as Spirit Is Everywhere

Yahweh's *ruach* is God's "divine presence" (Psalm 139:7, 23–24 NIV):

> Where shall I go from thy spirit?
>> Where shall I flee from thy presence?
> . . . . . . . . . . . . . . . . . . . . . . . . . . .
> Search me, O God and know my heart.
>> Test me and know my anxious thoughts!
> See if there is any offensive way in me,
>> and lead me in the way everlasting!

In the creative power of life, God is present. It is the presence of God that gives comfort to the people. Whether in hardship or in benevolent times, God's presence is always among us, and there is no place that we will not find God.

The gift and the presence of the Spirit are the greatest and the most wonderful things one can experience as an individual, as a community, or as a part of all living things. The Spirit is God's self, creative and life giving, redeeming and saving. Where the Spirit is present, God is present in a special way, and we experience God through our lives, which become holy living from within. We experience whole, full, healed, and redeemed life. We feel and taste, we touch and see our lives in God and God in our lives.[7] The vastness of God's Spirit permeates us all throughout our lives. God is uncontainable, yet our lives are encompassed through the Spirit. Thus, God's presence can always be felt through the power of the Spirit.

The Spirit is God. God is not something out there in the distant space but is present in our lives and in the world. God was always present in the lives of the people in the Hebrew Scriptures, as well as after the New Testament times. The Spirit can be experienced by all of creation—not just by Christians, which is what the church has said for most of its history. The Spirit is God's presence in the world, and the Spirit blows, breathes, energizes, and gives life to all of creation. The Spirit will take hold of us, and its effects will change our lives. As we move on to the way Jesus shows us the workings of the Spirit, we will come to see how the Spirit changed the world and Jesus dug the Spirit.

# Jesus Dug the Spirit

When I attended seminary, I was required to take two intensive courses in Greek, yet only a few Greek words have stayed with me these past twenty-five years. First among these few are *sophia* (meaning wisdom) and *pneuma* (spirit). It is no coincidence that the few Greek words I remember include terms from the two major areas of my own theological research and writing. The word *spirit* appears often in the four Gospels that open the New Testament, establishing a strong connection of Spirit to Jesus as we recognize the work of the Spirit in the ministry of Jesus.

In the New Testament, the role of the Spirit becomes better defined, more christological, and more ecclesial than in the Old Testament. The Spirit appears in the Gospel of Matthew, playing a role in Jesus' conception. I grew up with the story of Mary and the virgin birth and the statement that Jesus was conceived by the Holy Spirit (Matthew 1:20).

As a young girl, I had no idea what "conceived by the Holy Spirit" meant, because I had no idea how a baby was conceived. When I was five years old, I asked my mother, "How does the baby get inside a mommy's tummy?" My mother, never one to give elaborate answers, simply replied, "Belly button." The baby goes into the tummy through the belly button. To a five-year-old's mind, that was pretty incredible. It also made sense. It explained to me why I had a belly button.

I then asked my mom how the baby came out of the tummy. She again said, "Belly button." Wow! At that moment, I thought to myself, "I finally know the purpose of a belly button!" I was raised to believe whatever my mother told and taught me. It was very cultural. We kids were not supposed to challenge an older person. We had to honor our parents and our elders. I had no reason to doubt my mother. I never questioned my mom's answer and believed it for years. I just thought the belly button miraculously opened to deliver a baby. I was shocked to find out the truth as a teenager.

## Let's Do the Happy Dance

The New Testament shows the life of the Spirit as it moves and gives life to whatever it touches. The Spirit is especially active in Luke's Gospel, where it comes to Mary and to her cousin Elizabeth in the form of an angel of the Lord to provide new hope and energy for what the future holds.

Elizabeth was barren and wanted a child. Her hope of having a child diminished with every passing year. The desire to have offspring is more pronounced in a patriarchal culture, as a child carries on the family lineage. We

---

Every time you mention "a new hope," all I can see is a hologram of Princess Leia saying, "Help me, Obi-Wan Kenobi." That's a spiritual experience, right?

**THE DEACON**

---

recall the story of Abraham and Sarah in which an angel came to visit them and said that Sarah would have a baby in her old age. Sarah doubted this possibility and laughed.

In Korean society, the "prime age" to have children is one year after marriage. There's also an understanding that the prime age to get married is twenty-three. A girl is considered bronze at twenty, silver at twenty-one, gold at twenty-two, and diamond at twenty-three. When I was twenty-four years old and in the middle of my MDiv program, a Korean male minister used this timeline to explain to me that I had already passed my prime marriage age and was over the hill. He went on to tell me that I should have been married a year ago and should be pregnant now. As he was telling me, he laughed and poked fun at my single status. I felt such shock that the only response I had was to laugh it off.

Every culture has its views on the right ages for childbearing. In New Testament times, childbearing was for young women, not an older woman like Elizabeth. But hope comes to her when the Spirit visits her and gives her the good news. It appears that all things are possible through the Spirit. In contrast to Elizabeth, Mary is only a teen, and the Spirit also comes to her to announce that she will bear a child.

We see the role that the Spirit played in the conception of Jesus. The birth story tells of the power of the Spirit to upset the norm and the status quo and do something that changes humanity, making us powerful beings. It may be what Nietzsche described as the "will to power."[1] We become agents of change as the Spirit dwells among us and within us. We see this in the life of Jesus as Jesus walks on this earth and carries out God's ministry.

In a moment of fear, Mary finds comfort in the good news and can sing praises to God for the wonderful prospect of bearing a child (Luke 1:46–55).

---

**THE BISHOP**

She more than sang, she was saying, "Down with the patriarchy," before it was cool.

---

When something good happens to me, I do the happy dance. Not the cute little dance, but the crazy, dance-like-no-one-is-looking dance. When the Spirit of God came to Mary, she sang a song. When the Spirit came upon Miriam, she gave praises to Yahweh (Exodus 15:21). The Spirit elicits the joy and happiness that overflows in our hearts.

We know that the story of the Spirit and Jesus didn't end with the conception story. The New Testament says that the Spirit was in Jesus. The Spirit came upon Jesus, and it guided Jesus' talk, walk, ministry, and life on earth. The Spirit was in the life of Jesus, and Jesus' ministry was different than it would have been without it. The Spirit isn't enclosed in the life of the Hebrew people. The Spirit cannot be contained in the life of the wanderer. The Spirit is beyond capture, and it moves where it wishes.

## Jesus' Spirit-Filled Ministry

The word *pneuma* occurs at least 250 times in the New Testament in connection to the Spirit of God. Jesus' mission as described in Luke is a struggle, but it is aided by the Spirit, and even Jesus' disciples wait for the coming of the Spirit. The Spirit is powerful and will empower them "to be my witnesses in Jerusalem and in all Judea and Samaria and to the end of the earth" (Luke 24:49). The Spirit inspires prophetic witness to Jesus Christ, and it guides the apostles (6:10). The church participates in the ongoing activity of the Spirit of God.[2]

---

I'm not exactly clear on the word *pneuma*, but it sounds like this Rob Bell video my confirmation

**THE ACOLYTE**

class leader made us watch. It was cool and all, but I just wish he said things more straightforwardly.

---

As Jesus began his ministry on earth, he spent forty days and forty nights in the desert, fasting. We all know that fasting is not easy. It is painful, agonizing, and difficult. I know this because my mother made me fast as a child—just one day, but that was enough to let me know how painful fasting is. She made us fast every year on Good Friday. My mother would fast for three days, from Good Friday to Easter Monday, with only water to drink. For me, it is one of the most difficult physical things to carry out. When I fasted, I felt dizzy, lightheaded, faint, and worried, and my stomach ached.

If you have ever fasted, you've probably noticed that the hardest part of a day's fast is to miss the first meal. After your body groans in pain and want after the first skipped meal, going without the second meal is a little easier. But by midnight, you are faint and fighting the agony of hunger. Every year, we would have to fast, and it was a day that I anticipated with dread. For me, Good Friday became a day of pain. Perhaps my mother wanted us to know that, and that's why she made us fast.

**THE DEACON**

Once when I was a baby Christian, I fasted for forty-eight hours straight. I'm pretty sure I learned what I needed to learn in my spirit and haven't done it since. Now I just live into the jubilee feast.

One year, when I was nine years old and my sister was ten, we spent the morning of Good Friday in our small, two-bedroom apartment. Although we were hungry, we decided to venture out of the apartment and go to the back of the apartment building, where all the children usually played. My sister and I found fifteen cents, and thus it was a big temptation to go out. In the 1970s, you could buy candy with pennies. There were Sour Patch Kids candies for a penny, and I loved the Big Foot red jelly candies, which sold for a nickel, so fifteen cents to a child was like finding gold, especially when we were in pain with hunger.

Without debating whether it was right or wrong, we walked to the store. We bought fifteen one-cent candies and carefully divided them between us. Those candies were the most delicious thing we had ever tasted.

After my sister and I finished the candy, we immediately felt remorse. The candy nourished our bodies, but then we were covered with guilt. What had we done? Why did we eat this when our mother had told us to fast? It was one of the guiltiest feelings that I've had in my life. The rest of that Good Friday was horrible, and I understood what it meant to obey my mother and also to fall into temptation. I moped around for the rest of that Good Friday, wishing I had resisted temptation. To this day, I am convinced that I cannot resist temptation without the help of the Holy Spirit.

The Holy Spirit is the strength, the power, and the sustainer that prevents us from falling into temptation. Just look at Jesus in the desert. I only fasted for half a day and fell into temptation to fill the hunger within my stomach. But Jesus fasted forty days, and *then* he was tempted! Jesus was tempted to jump from the temple, to turn stones into bread, and to rule all the realms of the earth, but the Spirit was there to guide Jesus and help him overcome the temptation.

**THE ELDER**

I wish I had that kind of Spirit-strength when it comes to the ability to resist craft beer . . . or my more colonizing tendencies.

The Spirit is the powerful intelligence that fills the ministry of Jesus. The Spirit never leaves Jesus. It fills Jesus and helps him overcome the temptations that come his way. Jesus is self-aware of the Spirit, which empowers him and keeps him in the fold. The presence of the Spirit is felt during his ministry as he teaches and heals. It is present with the people. The Spirit nurtures Jesus and gives him strength to move forward.

I clearly remember my children's baptisms. Each was done by my friend Rev. Peter Ma. These rites were joyous occasions of welcoming my kids into the family of God. I dressed them up in the whitest outfits I could find. For my daughter, that was easy. She wore a fluffy hand-me-down white ruffled dress, white socks, white shoes, and a white bandana. For the boys, it was trickier. But I did find a white top and a pair of blue jeans for my oldest son. Then for my second boy, I found a knitted white sweater and matching white knit pants. (I know it sounds corny, but on a four-month-old baby, it looked adorable.)

Each of the Bible's four Gospels tells of Jesus being baptized even though it was anomalous, as he was a sinless man and didn't appear to need a baptism. The most intriguing part of the whole episode is when the Spirit descends on Jesus. The Spirit bears witness to Jesus by proclaiming his divine lineage and pronounces the godly identity of Jesus. The Spirit is a dove descending upon Jesus. Can you believe this? No dove descended on me or on my three kids when they were baptized, but we have a solid, tangible figure of the Spirit as a dove during Jesus' baptism. This is an incredible scene.

The Spirit is dynamic as it moves through the life of Jesus. When Jesus begins his ministry, he declares, "The spirit of the Lord is upon me" (Luke 4:18). At the most important times of Jesus' life, the Spirit is present and moving and changing. We feel the Spirit in the life and ministry of Jesus.

The Spirit is present at the fabulous appearance of Moses and Elijah on the Mount of Transfiguration. As at the baptism, a voice from heaven declares Jesus to be God's Son. At the Transfiguration, the heavenly voice tells the disciples, "Listen to him."[3] There is an intimate connection between the Spirit and Jesus. The empowering Spirit's presence is felt in the voice/breath, just as it had been experienced during the Old Testament. In the Old Testament, the *ruach* (spirit, breath) was the breath that breathed life into creation and that breathed life into the dry bones of Ezekiel's vision.

In the Gospel of John, the risen Christ is said to breathe upon his disciples and thus transmit to them the Holy Spirit as they are gathered together. The Divine within us is not exactly our own breath, but breath is surely the closest possible analogue to what we mean when we speak of the human soul or spirit. Breath sustains us even when we forget it. It is such a natural reflex that we don't even think about breathing—except when a baby is born.

**THE ELDER**

I can hear my Mom saying, "This sounds New Agey. Are you sure this is Holy Spirit talk? You should consult the Bible on this one."

I remember at the birth of each of my kids, I waited breathlessly to hear them cry. The baby's cry signaled that the baby was breathing. Even though I was exhausted and aching as I lay on the hospital bed, strapped to machines with my legs wide apart as the doctor sewed me up, I anxiously waited for them to cry. When I heard that first cry, I welcomed it with all my heart. However, after that initial cry, I have never wished to hear them cry again! It was dreadful to hear them crying through the night at the hospital.

Breath is vital to our existence, but our most important breath comes from God. Breath is the Spirit of God.

## Jesus + Spirit = True Love

The surprising story of the cross is that Jesus says, "Into your hands I commend my spirit" (Luke 23:46). The Spirit is a part of the story of the cross. The Spirit is what Jesus turns to before the death on the cross. It is a mysterious scene of how Jesus commends the Spirit and maintains his divinity and humanity. It becomes a powerful way of speaking about the Spirit and the presence of the Spirit.

The title of this section brings new meaning to the "Jesus is my boyfriend" songs played

**THE DEACON**

on Christian radio and in worship. I can hear the new Chris Tomlin tune now.

What are some of the things that the Spirit does in our lives? Well, it moves us and keeps us going. When we see the power of the cross as the work of the Spirit, which even moves walls, we try to be open to the new creative ways of being human beings and doing what is good. Not bounded by the walls of the church, the Spirit is God's eschatological presence and power to guide the body of Christ. The power of the free Spirit came to challenge us, and it indeed did so. The Spirit came to transform the world and do the work of Jesus. As Jesus left the earth, he poured his Spirit upon us to enable us to continue his work. The Spirit completes what Christ has come here to do.

In Luke-Acts, we see that God's Spirit is upon the people. The Spirit does crazy things. It came upon the twelve disciples. It made them do things that normal people don't do. The Spirit moved the twelve disciples to act and change the world.

Just as we are often unclear about the Spirit and the work of the Spirit, the people around Jesus were not always clear. Even the disciples were not clear about what the Spirit meant. In fact, many were confused. Toward the end of his ministry, Jesus promised his disciples that the Holy Spirit would be their constant companion, even after he left them. The Spirit would comfort the disciples and help and guide them. After the crucifixion and the resurrection, Jesus the Christ began to give the Spirit to the disciples by breathing on them (John 20:22). After Jesus ascended to heaven, he left the Spirit with the people.

In John 4:14, Jesus meets a Samaritan woman at the well, and he tells her that he gives the water that wells up out of the fountain of eternal life. He links water to life everlasting—not just life on the earth, but an everlasting life that goes beyond the grave. The image of the well-spring of life, the water that gives life to everything that is parched and dry, depicts the importance of how the Spirit can quench thirst. It also links the Spirit to the essential material manifestation of water. As the water of life, the Spirit gives life to the dying.[4]

A few years ago, I took my family with me to a conference in Brazil. We experienced extraordinarily hot and dry weather. One day, we were waiting in line in the hot sun for forty-five minutes to go up the mountain to see the statue *Cristo Redentor* (Christ the Redeemer), and my kids couldn't stop complaining about the long line, the heat, the sun, and why we had to waste time in line to see a statue that we could see from the bottom of the mountain. To make matters worse, we had no water with us, so we were thirsty.

My youngest complained the most. He kept saying that his mouth was dry. He mentioned that there must be something wrong with his mouth. I told him to stop speaking, so it wouldn't get so dry. But on and on he complained. I thought that once we got up to the statue, the kids would stop complaining. But once we got up there, there was an enormous crowd, and people were standing shoulder to shoulder. My children kept saying, "Can we go down now? We are dying of thirst."

As a parent, that experience really tested my patience. It was supposed to be a great day of going up the mountain to see one of the new Seven Wonders of the World. Instead, all we kept thinking about was how great a cold glass of water would be. We knew that once we drank a cold glass of water, we would be able to feel alive again. But until we got that glass of water, we felt doomed, parched, and hopeless.

The Spirit, the one who gives life, can quench the deepest thirst—the thirst of our souls. Jesus is the living water and gives eternal life. Jesus plus Spirit equals true love, a love that provides for us and sustains us. As the Spirit gives us life, it becomes the light for us to follow.

---

Okay, okay, I already kept thinking "Sprite" every time I read the word *Spirit*, but when

**THE DEACON**

you started talking about quenching thirst, I wanted that cola alternative in my mouth. Luckily, the Spirit actually delivers on the promise to quench.

---

## Afraid of the Dark

I was always afraid of the dark. I still am, but in front of my kids, I pretend not to be. When I first lived away from home, however, I could indulge that fear. After I finished the eleventh grade, I won a scholarship to study French at Laval University in Quebec City. It was great to be away from home and be on my own in such a quaint, beautiful city. I learned a lot during that time, made good friends, learned to be independent, and even learned some French. Every night, when I returned to my room in the dorm where I lived at the university, I would turn on all the lights, check under my bed, and open all the closets in my room and the drawers. This was my evening ritual. I just wanted to make sure nothing was in my room. Then I left the small desk lamp on all night. Now I travel a lot for my speaking engagements, and in my hotel rooms, I still leave the bathroom light on, just in case!

We all love the light. It gives us sight, warmth, and a sense of security. This experience of light is important for helping us understand the Spirit in the New Testament. There, light is associated with the Spirit of God, understood as the divine light. Light and life come forth from God. Jesus used light to refer to good works: "Let your light shine before others, that they may see your good deeds" (Matthew 5:16). Our good work is associated with bright things, and the possibility of our doing good exists because the Spirit is within us.

Light is part of God's essence, as is love. According to 1 John 1:5, "God is light; in him there is no darkness at all." Jesus states that he is the light of the world. The Spirit as light enables us to be a bright, shining light in the world—a light that fears no evil. This light can only be given by God. On the day of the Pentecost, the tongues of fire came upon the people in the upper room. The Spirit as light descended upon them. Light as fire filled the people in the room. It must have been either a beautiful sight or a very chaotic sight, with folks wondering what was happening.

---

So are you saying that if we want to get out of the dark, it comes at a Pente-cost? ;)

**THE DEACON**

---

God is the creator of physical light, as well as the giver of spiritual light, by which we can see the truth. Light exposes that which is hidden in darkness; it shows things as they really are. To walk in the light means to know God, understand the truth, and live in righteousness. We need to allow God's light to shine. Jesus is the "true light," which shines on us.

We see other biblical images of the Spirit as light. Paul encountered the divine light on the road to Damascus. There was a bright light and a voice. We, too, encounter the light. We search for the light and find that the light is within us. We allow the Spirit to work within us. The light within us is the brightest thing in the world. We need to embrace the light, which will help us overcome and conquer our own sinful ways. We need the light to reveal the way of living out the gospel. We need the light so we can move toward the light. Moving toward the light means walking with Christ. Moving toward the light means living our lives by the teachings of Jesus' Sermon on the Mount.

**THE ELDER**

I think my wife bought a Thomas Kinkade coffee-table book entitled *Moving toward the Light*.

The Sermon on the Mount is a guide to help us live the gospel, teaching us what it means to be filled with the Spirit and the light, a representation of the life that Jesus wants us to build. It provides a way for us to walk with Jesus in the light.

Light is powerful. It can nourish life. It can penetrate many things. In the Sunday school of my childhood, we sang "This Little Light of Mine," as did many other children. I used to teach it to my children. As director of Christian education, I taught it to all the children in our congregation's Sunday school. Some Christian traditions, such as the Religious Society of Friends (the Quakers), associate the Holy Spirit with light. The Quakers talk about the light of Christ and the workings of the Holy Spirit. The Holy Spirit is the light of the world. It is easy to associate light with goodness and the absence of light with evil.

George Fox (1624–1698), founder of the Quakers, lived during a time of social upheaval and war. He rebelled against the religious and political authorities. He preached publicly and soon had followers. He wanted Christianity to go back to its pure principles. One of Fox's claims was that there is "that of God in everyone." The living Christ continues to be present to guide our lives, as the Holy Spirit is the inward light. This is why individuals and the worshipping community can have firsthand experience of the living God. The Holy Spirit is also the spiritual basis for religious authority and the means of discerning the will of God. This understanding of God at work in the church is based on Acts 2, the account of the early church's experience of the presence and power of the Holy Spirit. Thus, the Spirit of God is not only experienced personally, but can also be a corporate experience for the community of faith. The Scriptures' promise is that upon Jesus' death, he would send another Counselor, an Advocate in his place—namely, the Paraclete (John 14:25–26). The Holy Spirit is a living experience of the Godhead. It is also a prophetic voice that can empower people to act and live out the gospel.[5]

Christ is the inward light that gives us peace and comfort. We who have the light in us need to share the light with others. We all participate trying to build the reign of God here on earth, and it is the Spirit that helps us build this reign. We experience the Spirit as we experience love, joy, peace, patience, kindness, goodness, and faithfulness. The reign of God exhibits these characteristics, as it is filled by the Spirit. Ministry is a gift from the Holy Spirit. A prophetic ministry is led by the Holy Spirit. The authority for ministry comes from Christ through the Holy Spirit. The Spirit helps us to move and engage in the ministry of Christ.

**THE BISHOP**

I'm ready and willing to empower this kind of Spirit-powered ministry in my diocese. We need more bearers of the light.

Howard Thurman, an African American Baptist minister, theologian, and civil rights leader, was influenced by the Quakers, which may explain his affinity to the understanding of Spirit as light. Thurman served as the dean of Rankin Chapel at Howard University, was the first African American dean of Marsh Chapel in Boston University, and was a prolific writer on ethics and culture, deeply influenced by Martin Luther King Jr. (who was in turn influenced by Thurman's writings) and other leaders of the civil rights movement. Thurman used Scripture to convey the character of Jesus. He noted that John 1:4 says, "In him was life, and the life was the light of all people." Writing about this passage referring to light, Thurman emphasized the life-giving aspects of the Gospel of John where Christ is understood as light. Jesus said, "I am the Light of the world; he who follows me will not walk in the darkness, but will have the Light of life" (John 8:12). The light is commonly associated with Jesus. But if Jesus is associated with the Spirit, then the Spirit as light also needs to be emphasized.

We need to be aware of the light that leads us. The inner light within all of us will lead us to become disciples who are empowered to do the work of justice. We need to allow the light to move us forward, so we can march against injustice and try to build the reign of God in this world.

---

I stand with this tradition. Marching against injustice is my new weekend hobby, ever since November 2016. Hmm . . .

**THE DEACON**

---

## The Lepers Are Healed

I traveled to India when I was a seminary student at Knox College in Toronto, Canada. When I applied for the summer mission student program, I wanted to go to Africa, and India was not on my radar. As luck would have it that my friend was chosen to go to Africa, and I was picked to go to India. India did not excite me at the time.

But that all changed once I got to India. I began to appreciate India's history, culture, and religious traditions. I learned to wear a sari and eat Indian food and appreciate the different tastes that the rich culinary palette has to offer.

It was also in India that I first encountered leprosy. I had read about it in the Bible but had no idea that there were so many lepers in India. At first, I just noticed beggars without hands or feet, but later in the summer, I realized that the beggars were lepers. I realized this when I visited Mother Teresa's Missionaries of Charity in Calcutta. There, the compound was filled with people with leprosy and many other diseases uncommon in the first world. They were being cared for by the sisters and by volunteers who come from around the world. With leprosy, pain will turn to numbness, and the skin loses color and becomes scaly. Sores and ulcers form, and one's voice becomes hoarse and husky.

In the Old Testament, leprosy was understood as a disease of the unclean; the term was used generically to mean many skin diseases, including minor ailments such as contact dermatitis and hives. During the Old Testament and late ancient times, the skin conditions defined as leprosy were thought to be contagious, so lepers had to live outside of the city walls. The Old Testament gave a clear way for dealing with lepers. Leviticus 13 states that a person suspected of leprosy had to have a priest inspect the lesion. Then after further examination and monitoring, if the condition did not get better, the person was declared ritually unclean. Lepers had to tear their clothes and call out, "Unclean, unclean" while walking through the streets. They were separated from family and friends and were often left homeless and without security. It was a wretched life, as they suffered physically, socially, and mentally.

These were the terrible conditions still in force when lepers decided to approach Jesus. There are two New Testament narratives of Jesus healing lepers. In the first, the Gospels state that when Jesus came down from the mountainside, large crowds followed him. A man afflicted with leprosy came to him, knelt before him, and begged him, "Lord, if you choose, you can make me clean!" (Luke 5:12). Jesus reached out his hand and touched the man. "I do choose. Be made clean!" (Luke 5:13). Instantly he was cured of his leprosy. Then Jesus said to him not to tell any-one. He said go and "show yourself to the priest, and, as Moses commanded, make an offering for your cleansing, for a testimony to them" (Luke 5:14). Instead, he went out and began to talk freely, spreading the news. As a result of this miraculous healing, Jesus could no longer enter a town openly but stayed outside in lonely places. Yet the people still came to him from everywhere.

---

I still don't know how I feel about these miracle stories from the Bible,

**THE ACOLYTE**

but I think I like Mother Teresa. Does believing in the Spirit necessitate I get down with curing leprosy?

---

The other leprosy healing story is the one in which Jesus cleans ten lepers. As recorded in Luke 17:11–19, Jesus was on his way to Jerusalem and traveled along the border between Samaria and Galilee. As he was entering a village, ten lepers met him. They were still at a distance from Jesus but shouted, "Jesus, Master, have pity on us!" When Jesus saw them, he had compassion on them and said, "Go, show yourselves to the priests." These lepers obeyed Jesus, and as they went to show the priests, they were cleansed of their leprosy. It was another miracle story. One of the lepers realized that he was healed and came back to Jesus and praised God. He threw himself at Jesus' feet and thanked him. Jesus asked, "Were not all ten cleansed? Where are the other nine? Was no one found to return and give praise to God except this foreigner?" Then he said to him, "Rise and go; your faith has saved you."

Jesus did something that was not permissible. The lepers were outsiders and unclean. Clean persons were not supposed to be near the unclean. Jesus' engagement in dialogue with the lepers was extraordinary—something that can only be explained through the Spirit. Jesus, filled with the Spirit, was performing miracles and healing people, and he wanted to fill others with the Spirit. A Spirit-filled person can approach an unclean leper with compassion.

Lepers represent the rejected and the despised. Their visible affliction, like the deformity Shakespeare ascribes to Richard, Duke of Gloucester, in *Richard III*, was a symbol of inner turmoil. Their condition was from nothing that they did wrong, but it suggested to those who saw them that they were spiritually troubled. In most cases, something just happened to their bodies. In our own society today, rejected persons are often pushed to the wayside. We make Asian Americans foreigners. We blame foreigners for social ills. We become afraid of Muslims and want to ban them or register them. We want to push them to the margins and leave them there. Those whose sexuality is not hetero, whose gender is not cis-, or who are of a different ethnicity than European are usually despised and treated as the other. These people are pushed to the margins of society and ignored. Racial differences are virtually treated as diseases by those living in "pure" communities.

In Calcutta, I was a fly on the wall. I couldn't move my feet toward the lepers who were being cared for by the Missionaries of Charity. I could not reach out to them, bathe them, or be with them. I was too afraid. This is how most of us are. We are afraid of those who are so different from us.

---

This will preach! But which one of my ministers will go for it from the pulpit?

**THE BISHOP**

---

I have come to realize that it is through the transformative spirit of love that people can approach, love, embrace, and perhaps even heal those who are pushed to the margins of society. The Spirit-filled Jesus healed the lepers. The Spirit-filled Jesus showed us how we can do the same and heal the broken people in our communities and society.

In Matthew 10:8, when Jesus sent forth the disciples with instructions to heal the sick, he specifically mentioned cleansing the lepers. Jesus had compassion on the neglected, the rejected, and the outcasts. Jesus wanted others to feel the same love and compassion for the lepers. This is the ministry of Jesus—to welcome those who are lost and rejected.

The Spirit empowers the weak to do the work of God: to feed the poor, clothe the naked, visit the sick, and heal the troubled. It empowers us to be intimate with each other and also to be in solidarity with those who are marginalized. It allows us to move toward goodness and make the story of goodness alive in our world. We need to be able to move toward social justice and work for God's love within this world.

The presence of God as the light is tremendously empowering to us. It assures us that the God of love, the Spirit of love, will always move us in the direction of hope, sustenance, and love. The love of the Spirit of God will keep us trusting God. It will help us have faith in God and the great love of the Spirit.

The Holy Spirit inspired the writing of the Scriptures, revealing the wisdom of the water, the breath, and the light. It is also at work in the world, leading people into the truth of Christ. According to the Scriptures, the Spirit is our principle leader and the one who heals and restores us.

**THE ELDER**

I like it when you mention the truth of Christ. Nobody will address the truth anymore. Too many millennials have a scaredy-cat theology.

# That Time the Spirit
# Knocked Paul off His Horse

Jesus promised his disciples, "And I will ask the Father,
and he will give you another Advocate, to be with you
forever" (John 14:16). His disciples then, and now, will not
be left alone. When the Holy Spirit arrived on the first
Pentecost, it was not a quiet event; the sound was as if a
great wind (breath) filled the room in which the disciples
had gathered in their uncertainty and fear. The wind
shook up those who had gathered. All the chaos continued. Tongues of fire appeared among the followers of
Jesus. And when they went outside to speak, those who
had come to Jerusalem from a wide variety of places heard
the disciples' speeches in each hearer's native tongue, even
though those speaking were all from Galilee.

**THE DEACON**

Talk about some pent-up linguistic frustration that needed to get out!

The first Pentecost would have been a dream for social-media enthusiasts. Tourists in Jerusalem would have hurriedly dashed off text messages to their BFFs on whatever served as iPhones in the first century. The ancestor of Twitter would have exploded. "Tongues of fire dancing all over #disciples #upperroom #HolySpirit." "OMG. Peter's preaching. He's on #fireforGod."

**THE ACOLYTE**

I literally want to set on fire whoever's Twitter account that is. Maybe if they had Snapped it, that would make more sense.

Acts 2:1–3 celebrates a powerful event of the Spirit coming down to inspire the followers of Jesus. The Spirit descended upon those gathered in that upper room in Jerusalem. This event marks the resurrection of a frightened group of people and the birth of the church. It was a miraculous, confusing, wonderful event. Luke had a little fun with us by playing on the word *tongue* (Greek: *glossai*) in his telling of the experience. He used "tongues of fire" to describe the Spirit's dance with the followers. He then followed that by observing that those imbued by the Spirit received the ability to speak in different "tongues." The NRSV translates this as "languages," but the Greek is the same word, *glossai*, in both instances.

The Holy Spirit has great power to move the people and the church. That first Pentecost seemed something of a bizarre day in the life of the church, but what a birthday! As Acts describes, the Spirit inspires the followers of Jesus to get out of the upper room and preach the good news in Jerusalem and then spread the word: north to Anatolia; west to North Africa, Greece, Italy, Spain, and Gaul; south to Egypt and Ethiopia; and east to Armenia, Mesopotamia, and Persia. The empowering Spirit moves the church to do the work of God.

One may suspect that a modern translator had some fun with the dual meanings of "spirits" when recounting how the onlookers believe that the followers of Jesus had drunk too much "new wine" in the morning. The infusion of the Holy Spirit into the first disciples caused them to act in a way that did not make sense to those who heard them on that day of Pentecost. The Holy Spirit had led the disciples ahead of the understanding of the people who surrounded them. As those in the crowd struggled to understand what they saw, some could only think that Jesus' followers were in what might be called a drunken state of grace.

Pentecost stands second only to the resurrection among the incredible events that give life to the Christian church. In fact, Pentecost can be viewed as the resurrection of the followers of Jesus. The Spirit, promised by

Jesus, did not raise them from the dead, but it did pour new life into them when they were frightened, disheartened, and confused.

---

**THE ACOLYTE**

So wait, Pentecost is like a spiritual resurrection moment for Jesus' followers? Should I take that to be historical or allegorical? Inquiring minds want to know.

---

The Spirit gives us life and moves us to do the work of God and bear the fruits of the Spirit. We cannot see the Spirit, but we can experience the work of the Spirit. The Spirit lives in us and inspires us when we are frightened, disheartened, and confused—states in which we often find ourselves. Pentecost fulfills Jesus' promise and the Old Testament prophecies (Acts 2:1–13). Pentecost established that it is the Spirit that will move the people to do God's work.

The first Pentecost was a moment in time and a moment that transcended all time. For the disciples, it was a transformative moment. The Spirit transformed the disciples and enabled them to begin their missionary work. One might say it was the event that changed Galilean fishermen into true fishers of souls. This did not mean, as it might be construed today, that right action became a free-for-all, enabling people to do whatever the unseen Spirit moved in them. The disciples still lived in a world where the laws written on our hearts (Romans 2:15) remain God's laws, and the actions of the heart can still be judged by God. It was the Spirit that enabled the disciples to do their work.

In the time of Acts, the believers already could recognize that the Spirit is the source of growth in the body of Christ. One became a member of the church through repentance and the baptism by the Holy Spirit (Acts 2:38). The believers understood that the Spirit makes the church grow, as well as giving life and beauty to the earth. The Spirit is the love that keeps the church alive: it built the church, grows the church, and sustains the church. Without the breath of the Spirit flowing through the church, the church will die. The Holy Spirit motivates the faithful to spread the word of God and to do what is right and kind and good.

## Paul and My Childhood

As we think about the beginning of the church, we cannot ignore the effect that the apostle Paul had on the church. Paul was not perfect, as he would be the first to admit. Writing to the Romans, he notes, "All have sinned and fall short of the glory of God" (Romans 3:23). Although his letters contain ideas that many of us find problematic today, the majority of the church, especially the Protestant denominations that came into being during the Reformation, recognize Paul's importance in teaching what it means to follow Jesus in community. Paul's clarifications on the law in Romans provide a steadying counterbalance to the exuberance of Pentecost.

My Sunday school teachers were obsessed with Paul and his writings. It seemed as though our lessons constantly focused on Paul's teachings. We were expected to know Paul's letters and even his biography, as told in Acts, including the period when he despised Christians.

---

**THE DEACON**

Yeah, some Sunday school teachers take it upon themselves to be enforcers of grace rather than distributors.

---

There was so much emphasis on Paul that every time a new student named Paul came to church, we would cel-ebrate, as if he embodied Paul of the New Testament. Paul was talked about constantly—in sermons, Bible studies, small groups, and other teachable moments in the church. Paul received so much attention that I sometimes felt as if Paul were God. One may wonder to what extent this was hero worship, as one may idolize Odysseus or Aeneas, the heroes of two great ancient epics, both of which appear to be echoed in Acts.

The man we know as Paul was also known as Saul of Tarsus. He was from Jewish parents in the city of Tarsus of Cilicia, on the southeastern coast of what is now Tur-key. When he was young, he was taught the trade of tent making (Acts 18:3). Paul was studious and knew the Jew-ish religion well. His enthusiasm for the religious estab-lishment may have led him to persecute the followers of Jesus. He even went so far as to travel with letters of arrest from the high priest in Jerusalem. It was during one of those travels, on the road to Damascus, that Saul was converted by a vision of Christ.

Saul was persecuting Christians, and it wasn't pretty. When we see the context of Saul in Acts 9 riding into Damascus, breathing threats against the followers of Jesus, we see something recognizable to the Christians who are persecuted around the world. We in the United States don't see Christian persecution, but other Christians around the world know that their Christian faith can lead to death. For example, during the Japanese occupation of Korea from 1910 to 1945, many Christians were persecuted. They were either put in jail for their faith or killed. This was a horrifying time for Christians living under Japanese colonialism and persecution.

But read further on in Acts, and see what happened to Saul as he nears Damascus. The writer of Acts says that a light shone from heaven and Saul fell to the ground. A voice from the light called out to him, "Why are you persecuting me?" (Acts 9:4). Saul asked, "Who are you?" and the voice replied, "I am Jesus, whom you are persecuting" (9:5). Saul was blinded for three days. What a conversion experience!

---

"Blinded by the liiiight! Revved up like a——." Wait, what does that song really say?

**THE DEACON**

---

Going from persecuting the followers of Jesus to preaching the good news is one incredible story. The bright light shone and changed Saul/Paul forever, and he went on to spread the good news. This shows the incredible power of the Spirit, which was witnessed by Paul and the people around him.

## Paul's Spirit Christology

From his dramatic conversion experience, Paul portrays a Spirit Christology as he ties Jesus to the Spirit. Paul's first letter is most likely the one we know as 1 Thessalonians. In that letter, he writes, "You became imitators of us and of the Lord, for you welcomed the message in the midst of severe suffering with the joy given by the Holy Spirit. And so you became a model to all the believers in Macedonia and Achaia" (1:6 NIV). This sets the stage for how he proceeds to explain how one behaves and what the role of the Spirit is in people's lives. In brief, Paul can imitate Christ because the Holy Spirit works and dwells in him (Romans 8:4, 11).

---

**THE ELDER**

Spirit Christology sounds like a nice try, but if you threw in a little more condemnation for the flesh, I think we could get along a bit more. #RecoveringCalvinist

---

Paul sees that Jesus is raised to new life by the Spirit (Romans 1:4) and that it is the Spirit who enables the believer to confess that "Jesus is Lord" (1 Corinthians 12:1–3). To be "in Christ" and "in the Spirit" are the same. Just as God and Spirit are the same, the Spirit cannot be experienced apart from Christ. If you find this just a bit confusing, don't be alarmed. In the medieval era, efforts to interpret ideas like these led to massive splits in the church between East and West regarding the nature of the Holy Spirit.

Paul develops the implications in Galatians 5:22 (NIV): "But the fruit of the Spirit is love, joy, peace, forbearance, kindness, goodness, faithfulness." The Spirit not only gives us life but also provides fruits that will allow us to be the light of the world. The Spirit is the one who will bring us together so that we can live with love, joy, and peace. For Paul, the Spirit, the gift of God, is life within us that empowers us to do good. Without the Spirit, the world cannot see what love is or what joy is. It is the Spirit that moves the world to glimpse the holy life, a life that is in God. This Galatians passage of living in hope and peace will bring together love and understanding. We need to love each other as God would love us. In our world of pain and suffering, this is a hard task to live into, which is why we are so dependent on the Spirit.

I remember Galatians 5:22 from Sunday school and how the teacher would draw a picture of a tree. Within the tree is where the fruits of love, joy, and peace will blossom and ripen. This image is a powerful one for me. As my friends will attest, I love fruit, and I eat it all the time.

**THE ACOLYTE**

If the harvest of the Spirit is fruit, then what is the seed? And are you saying that love cannot be experienced without the Spirit?

Fruit in a literal sense is essential to our physical life. And spiritually, we depend on the gifts of spiritual fruit that give us life through the Holy Spirit.

For the Christians in Paul's time and ours, the Spirit dwells in the believers (Romans 8:9), and the believers are expected to bring forth the fruits of the Spirit (Galatians 5:22) in their lives. The Spirit lives and works within people to do the work of God. We as the people of God must open ourselves to allow the Spirit to bear fruit within us. Without bearing fruit, we cannot do the work of God.

## Visit to Turkey

In the summer of 2009, I went on a trip to Turkey with my oldest son. It proved to be one of the most important theological trips I have taken. I had never dreamed of visiting Turkey, but when the opportunity came to go, I grabbed it.

I went with the Dialogue Center in Allentown, Pennsylvania, which promotes Turkish culture, religion, history, and dialogue. During that trip, we visited Istanbul, Izmir, Ephesus, and Cappadocia. Of those cities, Ephesus stands out because it was one of several places, including Corinth, Galatia, and Colossae, to which Paul or people writing in Paul's name sent letters. While I was in Ephesus, all my feelings about Paul boiled over as I wondered how he spoke to and related to the people living in those cities.

As I walked in the August Anatolian heat (over 40 degrees Celsius, or hotter than 100 degrees Fahrenheit), I tried to find relief in the ruins, as there were hardly any trees or other sources of shade. The paper-thin shadows thrown by pillars offered the only shade. My son and I could not stand in the shadow at the same time. Yet that thin slice of shade was a relief in the oppressive heat.

There in the ruined city of Ephesus, my mind went wild with Paul and his letters to the churches. At the time, I had finished my PhD and was teaching theology. But I still wrestled with Paul's sayings about women in the church (1 Corinthians 14:34, 1 Timothy 2:9–15), and I wanted to come to terms with them. Thoughts swirled in my head as I walked the cobbled streets on that hot day. We got to an area where the road was imprinted with wheel marks. They were probably chariot wheels, the guide told us. As we examined the road, I thought about all the different people who had walked and ridden on this road, just as today we walk different roads. As we do, we understand that life allows us to take different paths. It was at that moment in Ephesus that I made peace with Paul's ideas.

I understood in a visceral, experiential way that the messages Paul wrote to the Ephesians, as well as to the Christians in other places, had to be contextual. I looked at the dirt road and the broken buildings, the leftover columns of an era now gone. Whatever Paul said to the Ephesians was relevant to the people who lived in the place at the time the letters were written. That applied to all of Paul's letters. I live in a different world at a different time. I realized in a new way that the context in which the words of Scripture are written have to be taken into account. When we think about the Pauline letters, we may take their meanings literally. We may interpret Paul as if he wrote without context and his words stand true through time. But this is self-defeating. On the day of Pentecost, God breathed life into the followers of Jesus, inspiring them to speak so that people from all different lands could understand their proclamation of the good news. In a similar fashion, God breathed life into Scripture so that we may have life. There needs to be a communal reading and a communal understanding of Scripture that give life to all people of our community.

---

**THE BISHOP**

Could you send me a picture of the Ephesus ruins, so that I can tell this story next time I preach? We need more educated congregations who understand that context is key! Different world, different time is right! It's time to move into the twenty-first century.

---

God's breath is for the purpose of building up. It is for building communities and building the kingdom of God. It is a prophetic vision of the Spirit. This requires us to deconstruct our traditional understanding of Scripture. We must be able to read the text against the grain to capture the meaning of the difficult texts.

A Catholic friend said that she was never allowed to touch let alone read the family Bible, which sat on a covered table in the living room. Her mother warned all the children, telling them that the Bible was to be looked at but not touched. So my friend grew up knowing the importance of the Bible but not the content of it. The irony of her story is that she is now an Old Testament biblical scholar.

In other instances where people aren't familiar with the Bible, it is because they just don't read the Scriptures. A Catholic theology professor told a crowd of theology professors that Jesus taught us that "the last shall be first and the first shall be last." He paused for a beat and then added, "To my Catholic friends, this comes from the Bible." The room, filled with Catholic theologians, burst into laughter.

---

The real joke is that there was a room "filled" with Catholic theologians.

**THE ELDER**

---

The Spirit is clearly evident in the writing of Paul's letters, both in the seven letters accepted as genuinely written by Paul and in the letters attributed to Paul but believed by biblical scholars to have been written by others and published in his name.[1] But treating Paul as a hero or some form of demigod is often part of the problem. The story of his life provides part of the context for the letters he wrote or others wrote in his name.

---

**THE DEACON**

Yes! I totally know what this means now. I just read my first Daniel Kirk book. Go proto or go home.

---

## Body and Spirit

Sometimes, Paul isn't always clear about what he means by the Spirit, and we see different meanings of the Spirit. In Romans, Paul distinguishes between the Holy Spirit and his own spirit. It is Paul's spirit that preaches the gospel of God's Son (Romans 1:9), and it is Paul's spirit that is challenged and that may or may not be joined with the Holy Spirit. There appears to be a separation in Paul's thinking between human spirit and God's Spirit. This may be due to the strong Greco-Roman dualism that became entrenched in the rise and maintenance of Christianity throughout much of its history.

The Greco-Roman worldview often relied on dualisms that highlighted the distinction between two things.[2] These dualisms include heaven and earth, good and evil, light and dark, and body and spirit. In the book of Romans, there is a struggle between the Spirit and the body or flesh (8:1–17). Paul viewed the Spirit as good and the flesh as evil. It was the body that caused sin to enter the world. The things of the flesh are sinful, so the church needed to make a distinction between the Spirit and the body; the two could not be both viewed as good.

---

It sounds like Paul needs to read some process theology. He doesn't understand the perils of supernaturalism.

**THE DEACON**

---

I grew up in a conservative Korean Presbyterian church. We were instructed that anything that had to do with the body was bad and that we needed to concentrate on the Spirit. This emphasis was enforced so vigorously that we were prohibited from doing anything that gave bodily pleasure. That included drinking alcohol, dancing, engaging in sexual acts, and eating too much. We were not supposed to enjoy the body but rather grow in the Spirit.

---

This isn't solely relegated to Korean Presbyterian churches. It sounds like every one of my fundamentalist relatives who ever had to go to rehab.

**THE DEACON**

---

This strict upbringing, which reinforced this dualism, made it very difficult for me to embrace my own body and body type. My church kept teaching me to ignore whatever the body desired, and my friends and I were instructed to ignore any physical needs or wishes. This caused several of my Christian friends to be diagnosed with anorexia and psychosomatic problems.

In Western thinking, there is a separation between the Holy Spirit and humanity. Rather than understanding that God the Holy Spirit is with us, in us and among us, many of our denominations (excluding the fast-growing Pentecostal denominations) have made the Spirit a secondary person of the Trinity who is not involved in our lives. As a result, there appears to be a vast divide between us and God.

---

**THE ELDER**

I can draw them a diagram if they need help understanding the proper order of the Trinitarian flow. And no, it's not like an egg.

---

Centuries later, we tend to be dualistic, shaped by Plato's teaching of dualisms, which has been perpetuated in much of Christian thought and thinking. But if we move away from dualism, we can see that the body and Spirit are not opposite. They can be united. It is not either/or; it's both/and. This dichotomy has been pernicious, and

What about a fidget spinner? My youth minister said it's a PoMo form of "perichoretic contemplation," because that's clear.

**THE ACOLYTE**

it's time we reconsider how we view our selves in relation to the Spirit. After all, we are temples of the Spirit of God (1 Corinthians 3:16)!

We need more both/ and thinking in our churches. The only kind of "Nones" we need to be creating are nondual minds.

**THE BISHOP**

The church is reminded that to be "in Christ" is the same as to be "in the Spirit" (1 Corinthians 12:3). But most Protestant churches don't see this connection and have less focus on the Spirit. Let's now turn to the early church and how it tackled the Spirit.

4

# How the Early Church Got Hung Up on Christ and Forgot about the Spirit

I f I had to go back in time to any period of the church to live, I would choose the early church. It was a fascinating time of debates, arguments, growth, and theological nuances. It was one of the most exciting times in our church history, with the early church fathers trying to understand who Jesus was: was he divine, human, or somehow both? At the same time they were trying to figure out how the Spirit fit in the Trinity.

Something unfortunate happened to the Spirit between the time of the Pentecost and the second-, third-, and fourth-century church fathers. "All of them were filled with the Holy Spirit and began to speak in other languages, as the Spirit gave them ability," says Acts 2:4. At Pentecost, the crowd saw a lively, fiery Spirit with

**THE ELDER**

Well, if I had to go back in time, it sure as $h*t wouldn't be the Reformation. . . . I try to steer clear of the Münster Rebellion when I can. Anabaptists be cray.

power so strong it could burn down a house or launch a movement. As discussed in the previous chapter, the Spirit came down upon the followers of Jesus and gave them life, and tongues of fire burned on their heads. It was a wild and crazy day! For those not present in the upper room, the flaming tongues of Spirit seemed unimaginable. But it happened. The powerful, living Spirit of God came flowing down on the frightened followers of Jesus who cowered in the upper room for safety, giving them a new life, a new beginning, and a new future.

But somehow this Spirit faded within theological discourse with the increasing emphasis on Christology in the controversies leading to the Council of Chalcedon in 451 and the insertion of the *filioque* clause (Latin for "and from the Son") into the Nicene Creed by the Latin church. The Latin term, *filioque*, is to say that the Holy Spirit proceeds from both the Father and the Son and not just from the Father only. I will say more about this later in the chapter. The Spirit became the stepsister of Trinity, demoted to a being evolved from Jesus, rather than an equal partner. Christology took center stage, and the Holy Spirit, in the face of significant biblical scholarship, played second fiddle to definitions of the nature of Jesus Christ. How could this have happened to the lively and powerful Spirit promised to move, shake, and change the world? The excitement of Pentecost disappeared, and the Holy Spirit became sidetracked and ignored in the church.

---

I just want to say that I Chalce-don't think this was a healthy development. I'm newly noncreedal in how I think about JC.

**THE DEACON**

---

The reasons for this are understandable. To spread the gospel, the church had to figure out the meaning of Jesus' life, death, and resurrection for its own life and ministry. Jesus was born, lived on earth, and carried out a ministry. His witness posed a threat to the powers of his day. Those powers had him arrested and tried. He was then tortured and nailed to the cross. The powers sealed the borrowed tomb where he was laid, to assure that his ministry and life were finished. But by God's grace, Jesus was resurrected from the dead. The church had to deal with such events, and as the pressing issue of the day, the debates over Christology crowded out the Spirit. The powerful Pentecost Spirit was pushed to one side as the early church focused on Christ. Jesus and the cults of Mary, martyrs, and saints became central to the church's theology and crucial to the spread of Christianity into the pagan lands to the north and the halls of the barbarian invaders.

## The Christological Rise

The Spirit that empowered and directed the church's beginning, moving and giving birth to the church, did not actually fade away. Rather, the early church's focus on Christ downplayed the role and life of the Spirit. To understand this, think about a mother's experience of childbirth. She understands the deep pain involved in giving birth. It requires that muscles in your body—muscles you never thought existed—act together to push that baby out. Through the pushing and the contractions, every part of your body hurts and aches as it expands and adjusts to give birth. The birth of the church brought similar birth pangs, and the pain continues—sometimes sharp pain—as the church tries to grow and expand.

Even as early as the days of Paul's ministry, the church was struggling with the true meaning of Christianity. The disciples did not see Jesus return, as they had anticipated. They slowly began to die, sometimes killed as martyrs. Christianity was spreading into other parts of the world, provoking controversy over certain doctrinal elements and the fear of heresy. The desire for orthodoxy was growing, and the leaders of the new church had to work to keep folks on the same page.

During the christological debates, the early church grappled with the question of whether Christianity was a monotheistic religion (akin to Judaism and later Islam). Was Jesus divine, and if so, how did Jesus the Christ fit into the larger picture of God or the Godhead? The importance of trying to fit Jesus into the big picture of God took on central importance for the early church.

Maybe Jesus was just too #ZESTY not to spend a few centuries on?

**THE DEACON**

During this time, the Spirit was typically depicted as distant and otherworldly. The Holy Spirit was portrayed as separated from our human bodies. There seemed to appear a huge gaping hole or an abyss between the Holy Spirit and humanity, so deep it seemed they would never cross paths again. The rich experiential understanding of the Hebrew people's encounter with the Holy Spirit and the New Testament experience of Pentecost became lost within the early church's understanding of God.

Perhaps Greco-Roman dualism and its emphasis on rational thinking, along with patriarchy, are partly to blame. Patriarchy does not love sharing the God-head with a female vitality. Reducing the characteristics of the three personalities in the Trinity undermines the importance of the love between the Father, Son, and Holy Spirit. Without that love, the Trinity becomes sterile, a more comfortable notion for a patriarchal society. Additionally, in a world where rationality is valued over emotions and wisdom, it was easy to dismiss the Spirit, whose work moving people and making changes in the world couldn't be rationally explained. Patriarchy desires rational order and hierarchy, making it easy to ignore the movement and presence of the seemingly irrational, downplayed Holy Spirit.

**THE BISHOP**

Female vitality is central to a true understanding of God as Trinity. All this feminine Spirit-wisdom is *fire!* Wait—did I just make a pun?

The early church fathers were the earliest theologians, those closest to the authors of the New Testament. They claimed that their teaching came from the apostles, and they resisted new ideas or reflections on the experiences of Jesus in favor of staying true and faithful to what they understood as the transmission of the apostolic tradition. As people wanted to preserve the truth as understood by the first apostles, it became important to seek out doctrinal teachings that preserved the sayings of Jesus. Afraid of syncretism or any mixing with other faiths of the time, the early church fathers stressed doctrinal purity and fighting heresy, hammering out key teachings about Jesus, God, church, and the Holy Spirit—always with a focus on Jesus.

**THE DEACON**

There are some heresy fighters in my old church that I wouldn't mind hammering out.

## Memory Verses and Creeds

I grew up attending several churches, since my father felt it was his duty to expose his daughters to as much Western culture as possible. We went to Baptist and Missionary Alliance churches, as well as to our Korean Presbyterian church.

It was in a small Baptist church where I had to memorize Bible verses. It's always good practice to memorize Bible verses, but it's even better when the church gives nicely wrapped snacks as a reward for doing so! Once in a while, we got stuck memorizing difficult passages from Daniel and Revelation. But the little sandwich-size plastic bags full of chips, pretzels, and candy made it worth the difficulty.

---

But can chips, pretzels, and candy really give you enough energy to keep watch for the second coming? Seems like you got the short end of the stick.

**THE DEACON**

---

At the Korean Presbyterian church, we memorized the Apostles' Creed in Korean. Learning it in a language I was not strong in was difficult and particularly challenging, since it sounded so foreign to me. It was difficult to learn such awkward phrases that were not commonly part of my vocabulary. But memorizing the creed in Korean was not all. I also had to memorize it in English! I only managed to do it because my mother made me memorize three words a day. I think I was able to finally memorize the whole thing in five weeks. To my great surprise today, I can still recite it in Korean.

The early church created creeds so that the believers knew exactly what they were supposed to believe. The most important in relation to the Holy Spirit is the Nicene Creed, which declares that the Holy Spirit comes from the Father. In the West, as early as the sixth century, the Creed was often recited with words asserting that the Holy Spirit proceeds from the Father *and* the Son. This is the *filio-que* controversy, a principal division between the Roman Catholic and Orthodox churches.

The early church was intent on defining who and what the Son was. It was crucial that people understand the Son, and subordinating the Son to the Father remained a threatening heresy. For theologians in the East, the Father served as that principle of unity, giving birth to the Son and breathing forth the Spirit. By the end of the fourth century, Christian theologians had generally agreed that both the Son and the Holy Spirit are divine—a major development in the church's understanding of the Holy Spirit. Any understanding of the Trinity must assert that the three components are equal and all considered divine. However, even as they argued that the three are equal, they put less emphasis on the Spirit and more on Jesus.

Constantine, emperor of Rome from 306 to 337 CE, was the first Roman emperor to convert to Christianity. He called the First Council of Nicaea in 325 to reach an agreement among the many squabbles Christians had over the nature of Jesus Christ. Most Christians thereafter adopted the Nicene Creed as their statement of faith. This creed, Constantine and the church leaders expected, would unite the people and ensure that everyone had the same faith. It brought Christian orthodoxy and empire together as one union, believing in one God. In this way, Constantine made Christianity the religion of the "known world"; this common religion helped keep the people together through their belief in one common God.

Not sure whether I'm more stoic toward the Nicene Creed or the early-2000s rock

**THE DEACON**

sensation Creed. Both can be insufferable.

The phrase "one iota of difference" comes from these early church debates surrounding the identity of Jesus. The early church was so focused on settling who Jesus was that they continuously debated terminology. At Nicaea, two camps debated the identity of Jesus: Athanasius believed that Jesus was *homoousios* (of one substance) with God. On the other side of the debate, Arius believed that Jesus was *homoiousios* (of similar substance) with God. The church debated these two Greek words to understand more fully the nature of Jesus Christ—two terms that are spelled the same way except for the one extra iota (or *i* in English) in *homoiousios*.

Arius, who had a larger following than Athanasius, used a common slogan to get his point across: "there was a time when he was not." Arius believed that Jesus couldn't have been of the same substance as God, for he was created and was not always with God. If he was created, there must have been a time when he did not exist. In the end, the Council of Nicaea decided that Arianism was a heresy. The council declared that Jesus is of the same substance as God and has always existed with God, for a creature cannot save. This decision was significant to the church. It meant that Christianity was monotheistic and had one God. Jesus was divine, and the question of who the Spirit was had to be defined and understood.

Besides this major controversy over Jesus, the early church held smaller debates on the nature of the Holy Spirit. But it became clearer and clearer that the early church was much more fascinated by Jesus than by the Holy Spirit. The Holy Spirit kept being pushed to the back burner as the church refined the doctrine of Jesus Christ. The doctrine of the Holy Spirit developed a bit later and took longer to evolve during the early church period.

**THE BISHOP**

Or maybe it just took all the men making the decisions a bit longer to evolve.

## The Logos Group

The fascination with Christ was clearly evident in my own upbringing at our family Korean Presbyterian church, which focused on Jesus: who Jesus is, what Jesus did, what Jesus does, what we need to do to be like Jesus. The list seemed endless. Everything was about Jesus, Jesus, Jesus.

This was especially true of our congregation's Logos group, a deep Bible study for people serious about knowing the Bible in depth. If you were only a Sunday worshipper, you couldn't belong to the Logos group; it was reserved for those Bible-thumping, pray-without-ceasing, "holier than thou" types. This group believed that you had to think, pray, and center your entire life on Jesus. It was a super-religious group, and no one could criticize it or make fun of it.

That Logos group reminds me in a quirky way of how the early church ignored the Spirit and devoted their full attention to Christ. Our church, particularly the Logos group, was so focused on Jesus that I didn't even know much about the Spirit or the Trinity. We had pictures of Jesus all over the Sunday school rooms, and we had books with pictures of Jesus. We had coloring books of Jesus. (And of course, Jesus always looked like a blue-eyed, light-skinned European with blond hair.) Everything was about Jesus and nothing else, much as it had been in the early church.

The early church thinkers, theologians, and fathers had many disagreements and discussions surrounding the Spirit. They were trying to understand whether the Spirit was subordinate to or equal to God. There was also confusion between who Jesus is and who the Spirit is, as they tried to understand God and the Godhead. For the early church thinkers, the Spirit was not differentiated from the Son as a separate entity. Some thinkers viewed the Spirit as the *influence* of the Father, who empowers the

Son to act; this understanding could mean that the Spirit was something less than a person. With ambiguity and uncertainty about how to understand the Spirit and what its function is, the real difference between the Son and the Spirit remained uncertain until the end of the third Christian century, well after the Council of Nicaea.[1]

Christianity is a monotheistic religion, and we worship one God. To maintain a monotheistic understanding of God, it is crucial to get a good grip on the Spirit, God, and Jesus and their relationships. People fear polytheism. They think of the pantheon of gods that ancient people worshipped in the Greco-Roman period and get worried that any hint of polytheism will make God a false god. This was one of the challenges of the early church.

With this complication, many early church fathers struggled to fit the Spirit into their understanding of the Trinity. They tried many ways to figure this out. One idea among the early church fathers was the subordination of the Spirit to the Father, and sometimes even to the Son. Irenaeus was well known for the image of the Word and Spirit as the "two hands" of God bringing about creation.

At times, the Spirit is so complicated that it can best be explained through a simple proclamation. The Council of Nicaea stated, "And [we believe] in the Holy Ghost."[2] This affirmed that the Holy Ghost was to be worshipped. If God is a monotheistic God, then the Holy Ghost must be of equal standing.

Justin Martyr saw a close connection between the Spirit and the Son, and he opined, "It is wrong, therefore, to understand the Spirit and the power of God as anything else than the Word, who is also the first-born of God."[3] In other words, he believed that the Spirit and Jesus are the same thing, which reinforced a Christocentric Christianity.

Whoa, is that what y'all think that means? I ain't affirming no Ghost. Let's get back to the Spirit talk.

**THE ACOLYTE**

Tertullian (155–240) made a major contribution to the development of Trinitarian doctrine. He believed that the Trinity is the doctrine that distinguishes Christian faith from Judaism. The Son was distinguished from the Father and the Spirit, as there is an existence of three persons with one entity. Tertullian also believed that the Spirit is the body of the Word. He thought that the three persons of the Trinity share unity, which late creedal tradition refers to as *homoousios* (consubstantial). This means that God is one substance with three distinct persons.

Augustine, who lived from 354 to 430, struggled with the notion of sexual sin. Known for lusting after women and for being unable to refrain from sexual sin, he was a lively character who also gave the church important doctrines to struggle with. Augustine's interest in the Trinity was the unity of the Godhead. He believed that the Spirit can only be received in the church and that the Spirit is the Spirit of both the Father and the Son (John 16:13). The church became a required conduit to experience the Spirit, gain forgiveness, and receive eternal salvation.

Augustine speaks of the Spirit as *love* and *gift*. It is love, as it was the bond of love uniting Father and Son, and the uniting bond between the triune God and human beings.[4] Augustine affirmed the Spirit's divinity and was able to call the Spirit God, even though many

**THE DEACON**

Justin Martyr,
Tertullian, and
Augustine—oh, man.
Note to self: Google
*homoousios*.

of the early fathers did not. He called the Holy Spirit "Very God, Equal with the Father and the Son,"[5] which helped the church solidify a view of the Spirit as part of the Trinity.

For Augustine the Holy Spirit is also gift. It is the uncreated grace (*gratia increata*) given to humans. The Holy Spirit assists us in being and doing good; it helps us live out God's commandments. Grace is a gift from God, something we have not deserved. While we did not deserve the Holy Spirit's descent upon us, we are the recipients of God's grace and mercy. The Spirit is a gift given to help us live a full life. The Holy Spirit as grace moves us to build the kin-dom of God. The church has somehow lost this meaning of the Spirit as a gift to us and has lost the powerful meaning of grace in our lives. Grace embraces us and carries us through the good times and the bad.

## *Filioque* Controversy

If there is one thing that really killed the early church's focus on the Spirit, it may be the *filioque* controversy. *Filioque* is a controversial term that comes from the Latin to mean "and (from) the Son." In the Nicene Creed (325), the phrase is "And in the Holy Spirit, the Lord, the giver of life, who proceeds from the Father and the Son, who with the Father and the Son is adored and glorified." The phrase "and the Son" was added at a later time and does not appear in the original version.

---

*This* was a controversy in the fourth century? My uncle's unwavering attempts to "Make

**THE ACOLYTE**

America Great Again" at every family function are more controversial than that. Bring back *filioque*! Bring back *filioque*!

---

In the debate over the role and place of the Spirit and its relationship, two major groups developed. One insisted that the Spirit proceeds from the Father and the Son. The other believed the Spirit proceeds from the Father alone. Those in the first group sought to enhance Christology by subjecting the Spirit to Christ, thus allowing Christianity to center on Christ. Over time, this group prevailed. The *filioque* was added to the Nicene Creed. The thinkers in the second group came to be regarded as heretics and threats to the church. The *filioque* is included in the Nicene Creed as used by Western churches from the sixth century onward, but not by the Eastern Orthodox Church.

It was not until 381 that the early church began to recognize that the Spirit also is divine. Until then, it was unclear whether the Spirit was just an extension of Jesus and God. The full deity of the Spirit was finally established in the Nicene-Constantinopolitan Creed (381). To us today, this decision seems obvious. It is obvious because the Israelites had always believed that the Spirit was divine. They understood the Spirit as God and recognized its power. In light of this, the early church need not have spent so much time quenching the Spirit. It focused so much on who Jesus is that the concept of the Spirit became an afterthought for the early church.

Perhaps the Protestant church today would look different if we did not embrace the understanding of the Spirit proceeding from the Father and the Son. If this didn't happen, perhaps we could have had a less Christocentric Christianity and a more Spirit-centered Christianity. This could have led to a more welcoming and life-giving understanding of faith. It could have developed a Christianity that could welcome the diversity of world religious dialogue and be more welcoming of different cultures and backgrounds.

The early church's theological views of the Spirit are limiting and constraining in their understanding of God. But in the medieval mystics, such as Meister Eckhart, the Spirit was strong, and it was preached as a route to sanctification. We need to reclaim the life-giving Spirit, who vibrates and breathes new life into us and the world, the Spirit who becomes the light in a world still made dark by the suffering inflicted upon each other and the planet earth under the devastating actions of humanity, driven by the "ruler of this world."[6]

---

Meister Eckhart? You mean the convicted heretic? If you want to see some real medieval

**THE ELDER**

heroics, get me a 3 Musketeers bar so I can shove it up Eckhart's heretical sinus cavity.

---

**5**

# Some Medieval Mystics Got Jiggy with the Spirit, but then the Reformers Put Duct Tape over Her Mouth

How much church can one family fit in a week? My dad, who didn't ever want us to waste our time, always felt the need to fill our days with something. That something was usually church.

As a result, my church upbringing is composed of an interesting mix of Pentecostal, Baptist, Missionary Alliance, and Presbyterian. My experience of this unlikely mix of denominations has made a profound impact on my Christianity and especially on my understanding of the Holy Spirit. It seemed as if the Holy Spirit had a special personality for each denomination. Certainly, the Presbyterians and the Pentecostals have different experiences of the Holy Spirit, and Calvin didn't have much appreciation for aesthetics in life.

**THE DEACON**

> So are you implying that Calvin would likely be a Nickelback fan? 'Cause if you are, that makes me happy.

I grew up attending services in so many different denominations because my dad felt that it was necessary to expose my sister and me to as many non-Korean churches as possible, as church was the ideal place to learn English. Even though I spoke Korean at home and English at school, my English still didn't meet my dad's expectations. So while our frequent church attendance filled our time, it also gave us free English lessons. Furthermore, as an immigrant, my dad wanted to make sure that we grew up understanding Western culture and society. Not only did church help us become more adept in English, it also served as a means to acculturate us to the Western world. Besides our Korean Presbyterian church's Sunday service, my father took us to a Sunday-night Baptist service, a Wednesday-night Baptist service, and a Friday-night Missionary Alliance Bible study. It was a busy week, completely full of church events.

We lived in London, Ontario, but my parents loved to go into Toronto and Detroit to attend Pentecostal revival services. These were not the static and robotic Presbyterian services I attended on Sundays, nor the always-friendly

Baptist services I attended on Wednesday and Sunday nights. These revivals were quite literally out-of-this-world experiences. At times, they frightened me. I saw things I never saw in any of my other church visits. It was during these services that I first experienced the powerful effects of the Holy Spirit.

Shocked, horrified, and confused is how I felt at eight years old when I attended the Pentecostal church revival services. It was a baptism-by-fire encounter. These early and intense experiences of the Holy Spirit were frightening because all the adults were gathered together in one room for hours while all the other kids and I were outside the sanctuary in the huge fellowship hall, and I could only hear the sounds of what was happening in the sanctuary: yelling, laughing, shouting, screaming, and crying. As the adults were making those sounds, we kids were playing tag, playing hide-and-go-seek, and just having fun. We were a loud and rambunctious group of kids. But even amidst our own blaring noise, I could hear the adults worshipping in the other room.

---

This sounds like forcing kids to grow up playing outside of the asylum

**THE ELDER**

from *One Flew over the Cuckoo's Nest*. A little traumatizing, but also probably there were some good-spirited folks in there.

---

One day, my curiosity got the better of me. I quietly shuffled out of the children's room and walked to the worshiping room in anticipation. The familiar sounds became clearer, and I came face to face with the door that separated me and my parents. Without hesitation, I eased my face into the crack of the doorway and saw the answer to my intrigue. Inside the room, I saw people with their hands in the air, singing, praying, and crying out to God. I saw some of them lying on the floor, crying and shaking uncontrollably. A few were dancing around with no reservations, moving wildly. Some people were shaking so violently that they fell over. Many people were speaking in strange languages, which I now recognize as "speaking in tongues."

At the front of the sanctuary stood a man hovering over a microphone. I was not sure if he was preaching or praying, but whatever he was doing, it felt like he was mad at something, as he screamed every word he spoke. The things I saw that day terrified me, and I didn't know if I was actually seeing it or dreaming it. It was as if I had entered the twilight zone, where the definition of normal and reality were completely skewed. I didn't know whether I should close the door and run away or keep watching. As I was being tormented by what I was seeing, I heard the minister's yelling getting louder than anyone else's voice in the room. In the midst of all this, piano music was playing in the background. With all the yelling, I'm not sure what exactly the intent of the music was.

What I saw and heard was not like my other worship experiences. I was both frightened and curious—curious as to why they were acting wild and possessed when they entered the sanctuary, where they quit acting as functioning normal adults. What happened in that room that made those people act like that? Were they disturbed or even possessed? I could not understand. I tried to go back to playing with the other children, but I could not stop looking. And then, in the distant part of the room, I saw my mom with her hands held up high, eyes closed, with tears rolling down her face as she spoke in tongues.

---

This sounds kind of like the adult version of the documentary *Jesus Camp*.

**THE DEACON**

---

On the ride home, I could not summon the courage to ask my parents about what I had seen. Questions were not welcomed in our household, as I had learned after I asked too many "but whys?" Rather, I was glad that whatever had happened in that sanctuary made them feel much better, as they were calmer and seemed to be more at peace. After those revival services, we always drove home in better spirits than when we had arrived. Often I thought to myself, "If my parents are involved with this, whatever it is, it must be okay."

Still, in the back of my mind, I wondered if this was what Christianity was all about and what it would take to understand it. Like Shakespeare's Hamlet approaching the vision of his father, I asked myself whether this was the work of the Holy Spirit or some evil spirit that made the people speak in tongues and move around as though possessed.

From this early exposure to Korean Pentecostal Christianity, I did not want anything to do with the Holy Spirit. This childhood experience felt threatening and alien to everything I knew. I thought that if this was what the Holy Spirit is like, I should just move on to another religion.

These revivals occurred every four months. In between, I had more positive experiences of the Holy Spirit within my Presbyterian church—for example, prayers that included the Holy Spirit and the children's Bible study that mentioned the Holy Spirit. Unlike the revival services, these encounters with the Holy Spirit were comforting and warming. So I stayed in the church, not just because I had no freedom to leave, but also because I truly wanted to. I thought to myself that I could handle the strange experiences of the Holy Spirit every four months if there were also the comforting moments that came every week to offset the less enjoyable ones.

My early experiences of the Holy Spirit opened up my thinking to explore the many diverse ways in which many different people have experienced God and the Spirit. There is no one specific way to encounter the Divine. A part of Christian history that sheds some light on the work of the Spirit is medieval mysticism.

## Mysticism

Even though the early church emphasized Christ over the Spirit, the Spirit made a comeback in the medieval mystics. Mysticism is about the practices of visions, prayer, and the soul's mystical union with God. Mystics during the medieval period had wonderful and significant

Embracing the many manifestations of the Spirit is one way toward a unity that does not

**THE BISHOP**

dismiss diversity but rather, as Catherine Keller says, attends to difference and welcomes it.

encounters with the Spirit. These new experiences of the Spirit gave life to the Spirit for the world at large.

Some may fear medieval mystics. Their life experiences of the Spirit differ radically from ours. Their encounters with God sound so otherworldly and mystical that we are afraid to study them. But when we set aside our fear and learn about the mystics, their experiences of the Spirit provide a window into our understanding of God.

I still remember when a pastor at my old church told me that

**THE DEACON**

mystics were imitation theologians. Then I read a Richard Rohr book, and it made more sense to me than literally everything that guy ever said from the pulpit.

Mysticism deals with things that are out of the ordinary and elusive. To many of us, medieval mysticism deals with intangible experiences of God, which seem beyond our rational understanding. Mysticism may appear like the Pentecostal experiences of my childhood: irrational and otherworldly experiences of the Holy Spirit. Mysticism is about an unmediated space to encounter God. Within the early church, there was a sense that communicating with or experiencing God required the mediation of the church and a priest. But in the medieval period, the mystics found they could experience the Holy Spirit without mediation. Rather, the Spirit of God comes, and one can speak directly to God and encounter God.

**THE ACOLYTE**

Can't we all speak directly to God all the time? Do you have to be a mystic to realize you don't need a mediator to the Divine? Or does that make me one? Hmm . . .

Although mystical visions and experiences of the Spirit were present in earlier times, the medieval period in both the Christian East and West saw the emergence of rich and variegated traditions of mysticism.[1] These expressions of mysticism influenced the Christian faith and practices. Partly because of this, medieval theology of the Spirit shows intensifying diversity and spirituality. Theologians during the medieval period built on the patristic orientation, teaching, and theology, with occasional innovations.

The early church fathers worked on creedal formulations, including the *filioque* debate we considered in chapter 4. As we think about how our expressions of the Holy Spirit change and adapt to fit our location, keep in mind that the theology of the Holy Spirit has conformed to the different practices of its time.

As the medieval mystics emphasized the experience of the Spirit, their goal was the feeling of the Spirit. Revelations of the Spirit could take many forms and were not necessarily related to Christ or to the word in Scripture. Before the medieval mystics, so much emphasis was placed on Christ that the Spirit had been pushed aside. The Spirit was an afterthought to one's experience of God. The mystics put the Spirit at the center and core in their encounters of God. This centering of the Spirit swung the pendulum of Christian thought onto the work and presence of the Spirit.

While it was already agreed in the early church that the Spirit and God are one, it was during medieval mysticism that people began to truly experience oneness with

We've got to be cautious of an overemphasis on experiential Spirit stuff. The Spirit has a place,

**THE ELDER**

but we can't let our emotions run away from us, lest we lose sight of the kingdom work we have to accomplish. Christians, don't be so ecstatic you float away.

God through an experience of the Holy Spirit. And one did not need a mediator to experience God as the Holy Spirit.[2]

An exciting fact about the mystics during the medieval period was the increased numbers of women mystics. Up until this point, the spiritual writers or theologians of the church were men. Hence the early church theologians were called Fathers. Women were understood to be subordinate and subservient. It came to a point where, according to Augustine and Aquinas, women were viewed as incapable of experiencing and expressing the holy. But this changed somewhat with the medieval mystics—a development that provides a hopeful window through which modern women can become energized, empowered, and encouraged to engage in the work of God through personal experiences of the Holy Spirit. It gives legitimacy to women leaders in the church, as it shows that the Spirit moves in all of us regardless of gender and, by logical extension, regardless of any of the external characteristics the church has used, and uses, to exclude people from leadership.

**THE BISHOP**

My Julian of Norwich collection is extensive! I also carry around a hazelnut in my vestments just to remind myself that God is always my creator, protector, and lover.

We definitely need to see more of this in our time! Here are a couple of examples of some notable Christian mystics:

## Hildegard of Bingen

Hildegard of Bingen (1098–1179) was a German Christian mystic, as well as a healer, poet, visionary, composer, and theologian. Hildegard was sickly at birth, but from the age of three, she began to receive visions. Hildegard's parents decided to dedicate her, as an oblate, to the Benedictine monastery when she was about eight years old. At the monastery, she came under the care of Jutta, the abbess, who tutored several female pupils from wealthy families. When Hildegard was eighteen, she became a Benedictine nun.

---

Hildegard of Bingen sounds like a character from *Beowulf*. She must have been a badass.

**THE ACOLYTE**

---

Hildegard had visions all her life but at first was afraid to tell others in her community about them. She later did confide them to Jutta. When Hildegard was forty-two, she began to find her voice. She experienced a series of dazzling and visionary experiences, along with the divine summons to write and speak of her revelations.

Her visions were detailed, and she heard words spoken in Latin. She saw brilliant light, and inside this light, she sometimes saw even brighter light, which she called "the living light." While she had these visions, she experienced total loss of self.

Her visions were experienced through her five senses. She began recording them in the book of *Scivias* (Know the Ways), which took ten years to write. She wrote that she did not create these visions, but received them from God. Hildegard included the relationship between body and soul in the *Scivias*. Her mystical experiences of the Spirit informed her writing, her ministry, and her life. The Spirit was a powerful force in all that she did.

## Ignatius of Loyola

When I was a teenager, I had a super cool youth pastor, who mentored me during those rough years of development. As I struggled to answer God's call in some form of ministry, it was my youth pastor who encouraged me to attend seminary. He was a creative leader who tried different types of ministries. Among his diverse ministerial projects, he tried to incorporate a coffeehouse ministry at the church, to bring into the church children living in poverty who attended the neighboring schools. The coffeehouse was more than a place for coffee; it was a place to share ideas, enjoy musical entertainment, and gather for after-school programs.

One of the most interesting projects he started was to teach the youth about Ignatian prayer. Saint Ignatius of Loyola (1491–1556) was a Spanish priest who founded the religious order known as the Society of Jesus (Jesuits). The Jesuits served the pope as missionaries. Ignatius is often regarded most highly as a spiritual director, and he recorded his own method in a treatise called *Spiritual Exercises*. He taught a form of reflective prayer—a meditative and prayerful engagement and conversation with God.

My youth pastor encouraged us to practice this Ignatian prayer, as he felt that we would grow closer to God through this quiet, reflective, breathing form of prayer. Unsurprisingly, some teens broke out in laughter during what they thought was a strange breathing exercise. My youth pastor reminded us that Catholics and Buddhists are very good at deep-breathing prayer, but that this tradition is no longer present in many of the Protestant denominations. He reminded us that many people who pray use the breathing technique to draw closer to the presence of God. For when it comes down to the nitty-gritty basics of the Spirit, the Spirit is breath. If the Spirit is breath, we are breathing and praying the Spirit.

As a teen, I was eager to learn new ways of praying, so I tried to learn this type of prayer, using familiar techniques of deep breathing but a more focused concentration. It was a far cry from the noisy prayer that I witnessed from my parents during my childhood. Korean Christians like to practice corporate prayer called *tong song gido*. This is a loud group prayer that can last from ten to forty minutes. A minister leads the group or congregation into a *tong song gido*, and the members all join in loudly. Each person prays more loudly than their neighbor, so that they can actually hear their own voices in prayer to God. You can only imagine how loud and chaotic this form of prayer can be.

After months of trying, I became more comfortable, and I was able to enjoy my time of prayer. I also came to realize that one does become closer to the Divine through this deep-breathing exercise. In that moment, I recognized the connection between breath and the Spirit of God.

Breath is the invisible icon of the Divine. In breath-centered meditation, one rests the mind in the breath, returning again and again to the breath as the mind wanders. The breath draws one back to awareness and presence. In Christian meditation, it is the breath that draws one to the awareness of God. To speak of our human breath is a reminder of God's presence and becomes a way for us to be drawn toward God's presence at any time and place. Breath is like an invisible thread connecting God and us. The practice of remembering the breath and returning to it becomes a way of remembering and returning to God's presence.[3]

---

**THE BISHOP**

Some even say the Tetragrammaton (YHWH) is actually the sound of breathing, so God's name is our very breath.

---

Breath is essential to vocal vibrations, and in some ways, life is about having the right pitch. It is about connecting with others through the movement of vibrations and also giving off the right vibes. Even Pope Francis asked reporters who do not pray to at least send him "good vibrations."[4]

Vibrations are not meaningless; they are filled with meaning and provide answers about how things work in the world. The universe is full of vibrations, and vibrations exist in all aspects of life. The divine particle exists in all things. Spirit as vibration keeps us in motion, builds relationships, gives us new life, and sustains our life. We allow the Spirit to vibrate through us, so that we can become the instruments for God, and breath is essential to vibration.

---

So are you saying that
God is the Divine
Vibrator?

**THE DEACON**

---

## The Reformers Take On the Spirit

As we move into the time of the Reformation, we find a different pattern of understanding and experiencing the Spirit than the common understanding assumed during the medieval era. For the Reformers, the understanding of the Spirit wasn't as explicit as it was with the mystics. The Reformers understood and experienced the Spirit as tied eternally to the Word (Jesus Christ, Scripture, and preaching). One knows the Spirit or experiences the Spirit through the Word. For the Reformers, the Word was powerful. The Word moves people and transforms the world. They believed that one can come to know the Spirit only through the Word. This was like a return to the early church, where Christianity was Christocentric.

---

**THE DEACON**

I wonder if any of the Reformers ever read John 5:39 and following.

---

Luther and the other Reformers emphasized the intimate connection and relation of Word and Spirit. The Spirit points to Jesus Christ, as Christ is known through the witness of the Scriptures. Word and Spirit are inextricably tied up together. The Word describes the work of the Holy Spirit—active in the church and the ministry. The purpose of the Spirit, who indwells all believers and the church, is to lead the church into mission and ministry and to form the lives of Christian believers. The Spirit comes through the Scriptures and the preaching of the Word—not through the whole sacramental structure of the church (as in medieval Catholicism).

Reformers including Luther and Calvin maintained this relationship of Word and Spirit. They believed that the Spirit of God is free but maintained that God has established the Word in Scripture as divine revelation and the means by which humans can know God (through Jesus Christ). The Spirit "brings the Scripture alive," enabling people to believe Scripture is the Word of God and that Jesus Christ is the Son of God. So the Spirit is active with the Word.

The Word helps us interpret and understand the Spirit. Scripture teaches us what the Spirit is like and

So are you saying that the Spirit is an enabler for Reformed people's views on Scripture? Hmm.

**THE DEACON**

what the Holy Spirit wants us to do. Scriptures tells us what the "fruits of the Spirit" are. The New Testament church had a lively sense of the Spirit's guidance for mission and ministry. In so many ways, we would be lost without the Word. For example, there would be no way to know who the Spirit is or what kind of life the Holy Spirit of God is calling the church to live. The Word gives guidance on the nature of the Spirit. Furthermore, the Word sheds light on the Spirit's work in the church and in lives of Christian believers.

A basic principle for the Reformers was that in this relationship of Word and Spirit, the Spirit will never lead us to behave in ways that are contrary to the Word. For example, there was an incident in Texas where a mom, Deanna Laney, killed her boys by smashing their heads with a rock. Laney believed that God had told her the world was going to end and "she had to get her house in order," which included killing her children.[5] We know of others who also believed that God told them to do terrible things. For Luther and Calvin, it was clear that this could not be the Spirit of God, as the Spirit of God never leads us in ways that are contrary to the Word of God in Scripture. The importance of the Word is upheld. One must know and understand the Word, or else one would never know whether what one thinks the Spirit is telling one to do is really the Spirit of God or one's own misperceptions and feelings.

We know of friends and others who have often misperceived their own thoughts and presented them as what God wants them to do. When I was in college, I was dating a nice guy. I broke it off once but then felt bad, and we got back together. After we got back together the second time, I felt that it wasn't the right relationship, so I broke it off a second time. It was then that my ex-boyfriend told me that he needed to have a serious conversation with me. He looked me in the eye and said that God had told him to marry me. That spooked me, and I broke up with him (again). I guess he heard God wrong.

---

**THE DEACON**

I'm glad you kissed dating that guy good-bye.

---

Luther felt that many of his contemporaries had upset this balance of Word and Spirit by emphasizing the Spirit and downplaying the Word. There was too much focus on the Spirit without even understanding or reading of the Word. The result was making the Spirit independent of the Word. Calvin saw the same tendencies in the Anabaptists. As a result, neither of them sought mystical experiences of the Spirit. They decided that it wasn't for them and that there needed to be movement away from the separation of the Spirit and the Word. There needed to be solid connection between the two; otherwise, we run the danger of claiming nonsense or irrational perceptions and feelings as a message of the Spirit.

---

Why am I not surprised two dudes obsessed with the Word of God were trying to downplay the feminine breath of the Spirit?

**THE DEACON**

---

Thus, Luther and Calvin emphasized the work of the Holy Spirit as helping believers interpret the Word. As the Spirit helps the church interpret the Word, this in turn empowers the church to carry out God's will and work, as it is revealed in the Word. The great "freedom" of the Spirit is to be at work in ways we do not anticipate or even understand. The Spirit leads us in new ways of mission and ministry and strengthens our relationship with God in Christ, and with others.

## The Spirit Points to Jesus

The Spirit comes in relation to the Word to form the Christian's life and to lead and guide the Christian (and the church) in service to God in Christ. With the emphasis on the Word, rather than just keeping the Spirit as a stand-alone, there was a return to an emphasis on the maleness of God and Jesus the incarnate Word. Jesus was always associated with the Word, and the Reformers' emphasis on the Word led to a male-centered understanding of God.

Luther believed that it is through Scripture alone that we can come to an understanding of God. Reformation leaders taught that Scripture should be read by all, not just by the priests. This was part of the motivation for Luther and others to translate Erasmus's Greek Bible into German and other vernaculars. It was the holy word, and everyone, not just the priests, needed to have access to it.

---

**THE ACOLYTE**

My confirmation teacher said *sola scriptura* is what Bible bashers use to justify their bibliolatry. I'm not exactly sure what that means, but it sounds right.

---

In the Reformation's movement toward Christocentric theology, the Reformers understood the Spirit to function as a witness that proclaims Jesus Christ to us. This means the Spirit points not to itself but to Jesus (John 14:26; 15:26; 16:7). This concept has stayed with many of us within the Reformed churches. During our worship, the readings, prayers, and sermons all point to Jesus Christ. There is not much mention of the Spirit, unless one belongs to the Pentecostal or Holiness tradition. The mainline churches have tended to squelch the movement and power of the Spirit, as they focus on the one to whom the Spirit points, Jesus Christ.

In the morning, when
I rise, give me Jesus.
Boom.

**THE ELDER**

Those of us who were raised with these practices and teachings become afraid to say anything about the Spirit. We get scared and want to drop the subject of the Spirit, because it feels too hokey-pokey and irrational. We like to be able to explain things with logic and to do things in decent and good order.

I once visited a mostly white Presbyterian Church (USA) congregation. It was a traditional church with a focus on the word of God in Scripture. The church had a Communion service on the Sunday I was there. The Communion was carried out with such precision that there was no room for error or spontaneity. It was the most precisely timed Communion service in which I have participated. It was done so "decently and in good order" that there was no room for the movement of the Spirit to come into the service. This service reminded me of what the Reformers did with the Spirit: they put a gag over her mouth.

## Calvin's Church

During a meeting at the World Council of Churches in Geneva, the group I traveled with went to visit Calvin's church, Saint Pierre Cathedral. As an ordained Presbyterian minister, I was super excited to see the church that Calvin had attended and where he had preached. It was something I had never imagined doing when I was a

seminary student taking courses on Calvin and his importance to Presbyterianism.

When we got to the outside of the church, my heart
was beating fast, and I felt like a little child about to receive
a huge gift. The outside of the cathedral is overbearing,
with tall pillars. It actually looks like a courthouse, rather
than a church. Inside, the cathedral is massive, with high
ceilings and rows of pews facing the altar. We walked up
the long aisle and approached the high pulpit from which
Calvin preached. On the left of the pulpit was the most
fascinating part of the visit: a small chair that had belonged
to Calvin.

---

**THE ELDER**

Small chairs make me
uncomfortable.

---

John Calvin stated, "The highest proof of Scripture
is uniformly taken from the character of him whose word
it is."[6] This is sometimes called the "inner witness of the
Holy Spirit" to the truth of Scripture. For Calvin, the
power of the Spirit is special and can be more valuable
than all the reasons put together. The Word will not find
room in a person's heart unless the heart is sealed by the
inward testimony of the Spirit. The Spirit, who has spoken through the mouths of the prophets, must penetrate
into our hearts.

Calvin believed that the Holy Spirit teaches us a
spiritual understanding of Scripture, as Scriptures witness

God's Word. For Calvin, "Scripture will ultimately suffice for a saving knowledge of God only when its certainty is founded upon the inward persuasion of the Holy Spirit."[7] Spirit moves us to come to know God and it is indispensable. Thus it is only by the Spirit that Jesus Christ will mean anything to us. We can only come to faith by the Spirit. The Holy Spirit is the source of our sanctification, and our growth in faith. It is a sign that God is within us.

John Calvin said the Spirit is "the key that unlocks for us the treasures of the Kingdom of Heaven."[8] The Spirit will never leave us or desert us, since we are "marked with the seal of the promised Holy Spirit" (Ephesians 1:13). As Calvin said, "When we have received the Spirit of God, we have God's promises confirmed to us, and we are not afraid that He will retract."[9] We are united to Christ because of the Spirit.

The medieval mystics experienced the Spirit in their everyday lives and showed us that the Spirit influences us daily. In addition, the female mystics showed that women also can be leaders in the church. This understanding of the Spirit changed as time passed and the Reformation leaders entered the picture.

In different ways, the Reformers carried on the notion of the importance of the Spirit, which was emphasized by the medieval mystics. But the difference was now that the Spirit was viewed primarily rationally rather than an experientially. It was tied to the Word and not to wisdom.

The Reformers believed that the Holy Spirit enables ministries in the church. The purpose of the Holy Spirit—after the day of Pentecost—is to be God present with and in the church as the church carries out ministries of Jesus Christ. So the Spirit is never an end but always a beginning. The Spirit enables and empowers the church to serve the gospel.

Because they linked Spirit to Word, the Reformers essentially quenched the wondrous, gushing power of the Spirit. People moved away from the mystics' experiential encounter of the Spirit to a more rational understanding and encounter of the Spirit tied to the Word. The result during the Reformation was that the Spirit was slowly removed from prominence and became "quieter" within the church. The silence is reflected in current church practice, worship, and living, especially in churches that trace their heritage to the Reformation.

**THE BISHOP**

And we are still reaping the consequences of this tying of the Spirit to the Word in the West. We've lost the heart of our Christianity. It's time to breathe new life back in.

**6**

# Twentieth-Century Feminists Rescue the Spirit!

Women should rule the world. Have you ever wished that? I have. What would it be like then? Certainly the world we know today would see many changes. Would it be a better place than it is now? (Of course.) One thing is certain. Theology would be much different from what we read today if there were more women theologians around. Masculine language would be replaced by feminine or gender-neutral language. The male person of God would be out. The female spirit of God would be in. We would have a much different Christianity if we had allowed women's voices and global voices around the world to be heard in theology.

In addition, there would not have been so much sexism and patriarchy in the church if women theologians were allowed a voice and women interpreted Scripture.

109

The lack of diverse voices who were allowed to do biblical hermeneutics has caused a lot of pain and division within the church body. It has allowed patriarchy, sexism, racism, slavery, colonialism, xenophobia, homophobia, and able-ism to exist within Christianity. It has been detrimental to Christianity. Furthermore, feminist eyes would bring an added richness to this discussion of the Holy Spirit. We need more people around the theological table to bring newer dimensions and understandings to the narrow white patriarchal scope of the Holy Spirit.

**THE BISHOP**

This is amazing. I feel like I'm listening to myself at every denominational panel I've ever been a part of. Are we the same person?

Let's look back at the story of the Spirit throughout our church history. What does feminist theology say about it? The early Christian communities consistently spoke of the Spirit as the motherly, regenerative breath and power of God within creation. They believed that the Hebrew feminine name of the Spirit, *ruach*, was a linguistic clue to certain woman-specific characteristics of God as Spirit. As these early Christians rightly understood that God transcends gender, their point was not that God is a female deity, but that it is appropriate to refer to God's mystery, love, and power in both male and female terms.

However, most of our *church fathers* (isn't that a dead giveaway to the foundations of parochialism?) have a patriarchal perspective on the Holy Spirit. Patriarchal pneumatology[1] applies the neuter Greek word for breath, *pneuma*, contrasting with *sophia*, the feminine Greek word for wisdom in the Septuagint, which is the primary Greek translation of the Old Testament. The sexless pneumatology began with the early church fathers and dominated Christian history and thought up to the 1960s, when theologians including Gustavo Gutiérrez opened the door to marginalized voices around the world, especially Latin American, African, Asian, and female theologians. This challenged the patriarchal understanding of the Holy Spirit—a constricting perspective that ignores all visceral experience, including women's experiences and understanding of the Spirit.

One of the dismal "discoveries" in the feminist rereading of the philosophical tradition was the extent to which Locke, Rousseau, Kant, Hegel, Schopenhauer, Marx, and other canonic modern thinkers perpetuated patriarchal assumptions about women, sex, and gender. The conceptual binaries of the premodern philosophical tradition did not disappear but were recast in terms that continued to associate the male with reason and culture, and the female with emotion and nature.[2] The first real breakthrough came only at the end of the nineteenth century with the work of Friedrich Nietzsche and Sigmund Freud.[3]

## My Patriarchal Father

My father epitomized the patriarchal "person in charge." I grew up fearing his anger and wrath. He was a small,

**THE DEACON**

Yeah, gender binaries are about as helpful in postmodernism as trying to tell your Evangelical friends that you just read a book called *Organic Marxism* by your favorite Christian theologian.

thin, feeble-looking man, an inch shorter than my mother (who was viewed as a very "tall" Korean woman). So, seeing my father, one would say he looked harmless, gentle, and kind. In fact, this was the persona he presented to the world. At home, however, he ruled the family with strong patriarchal rule of obedience and subordination. Not only was it necessary that my sister and I obey him, but in addition, my mother, all his sisters (my aunts), and even his mother (my grandmother) were expected to live under his rule. In my father's frame of mind, God created men to rule over women. Women are to obey their husbands and their brothers and fathers. If they do, then good things will happen, and God will bless them. This was my father's gospel, and he would often preach it to strangers, family, and neighbors.

My experience of patriarchy was not limited to my family. It was common in my church, too. The church of my youth preached only a white, male God who would save us poor women. The church talked about the maleness of God and the subordination of women not only in society but also in the church. This patriarchy was so embedded in my life that it was easier to resign myself to it than to fight it, at least throughout most of my childhood and youth. Only in my later teens did I begin to search for a more equitable way of understanding humanity and God. Much of my search occurred at Knox College, a Presbyterian seminary in Canada, where a few professors challenged me to read feminist thinkers and theologians.

---

## #MaleFail

**THE ACOLYTE**

---

This continued through my PhD program, where I studied feminist theology and found hope in new ways of talking about a feminine understanding of the Divine. Throughout my search, I was comforted to find feminist theologians rescuing the Spirit from the cages of patriarchy. Several feminist theologians have worked on or are writing about the Spirit with provocative insights, interesting and full of surprises, creating excitement about the possibilities and how they change and move us. It is to some of these feminist theologians that we now turn.

## Meeting Elizabeth A. Johnson

I met Elizabeth A. Johnson in 1994, when she was an invited speaker at the University of Saint Michael's

College, where I did my PhD. I idolized her, and I was excited to hear and meet her. She was shorter than I had imagined, and her voice was gentle and soft. I had enjoyed her work so much that to hear her talk was like listening to a rock star. Listening to her opened up an entirely new way of looking at the world.

Johnson's work has continued to be informative and has influenced my own work, endlessly informing, challenging, and redefining my theology. For example, Johnson presents a gender-inclusive understanding of the Spirit. She lays out a feminine Spirit-Sophia as the divine person who opens up the mystery into Jesus-Sophia and Mother-Sophia. Spirit-Sophia accompanies human beings in encountering the Trinitarian mystery. Johnson highlights the equality of the divine Spirit within the Trinity and how the Spirit creates communion within God. This new perspective on the Trinity brings fresh life into the old Trinitarian conversations.

I was actually going to name my daughter Trinity. I was pregnant during the time I was writing my PhD thesis and also during the time when the *Matrix* movies were coming out. I really loved the movies and the feminine character of Trinity, as played by Carrie-Anne Moss. She was a powerful, passionate, and beautiful character. I wanted my girl to be just like the Trinity of *Matrix*. Then I got worried about using a nontraditional name and decided to name her Elisabeth. Whenever I mention to my daughter that I was going to name her Trinity, she's grateful that I named her Elisabeth instead.

For Elizabeth A. Johnson, the Spirit literally means a blowing wind, a storm, a stream of air, breath in motion, or something in motion, impossible to pin down. One

Elisabeth and Trinity
both seem like perfectly
rock star names to me.

**THE DEACON**

cannot put Spirit on a platter and say, "This is the Spirit."
The Spirit can't be held down to present as a tableau. It is
constantly moving like a rushing wind; you never know
which way it is going to flow. This unknowingness points
us toward the mystery of God as Spirit. In feminist theology, there is room for mystery, which felt absent in the
rational thinking of the Reformers and male thinkers
before them. In the suffering of women, we can bring a
liberative perspective to the Holy Spirit.

The Spirit is the sense we feel of the living God, who
creates, sustains, and guides all things. Divine Spirit is the
creative and freeing power of God let loose in the world.
It is a dynamic term that captures a universal perspective
and shows us something about divine activity in the world.
What we witness on earth is the movement of the Spirit.
In Sunday school, I was taught that God is far above us,
on a throne, and that the Spirit is otherworldly, beyond
our realm. Until I was transformed by reading feminist
work, I never recognized that God is in our midst and in
our lives.

The gender of a noun is significant, as it often molds
our thoughts. This is far more obvious in languages such
as Hebrew, Greek, Latin, French, and German, where all
nouns are masculine, feminine, or neuter. The Hebrew
word for Spirit, *ruach,* is feminine, and the biblical Greek
equivalent, *pneuma*, is neuter. The common Latin term,

*spiritus*, is masculine. The biblical translator Jerome figured that these terms together signify that God transcends all categories of sexuality, and Spirit is neither male nor female.[4] This was a significant move, which was not fully embraced until feminist theologians wanted to move away from the masculine understanding of God.

---

**THE ELDER**

Every time you say "neuter," I can't help but think of Bob Barker.

---

In the Hebrew Scriptures, *ruach*'s activities are wrapped around women's historical reality. The Spirit creates new life, works to sustain it in many ways, and heals what has been damaged. Scripture uses a range of imagery to speak about these deeds, such as the water that cleanses and refreshes, the fire that warms and brightens, the cloud that cools, and the wind that blows free. One such image for spirit centers around the symbol of the bird, a symbol of a female deity in ancient Near Eastern religions. For example, Nekhbet, an early Egyptian goddess who is "the Mother of Mothers," is represented by a vulture signifying eternity.

My dad loved animals and birds. In our backyard in Korea, when I was a little girl, we had a huge cage the size of a three-car garage, with various birds in it. My dad liked all animals, but my mother was selective. She liked animals that were in tanks (like fish) or cages (like birds).

When we immigrated to Canada, we lived in an old six-story apartment building. We lived on the sixth floor and our apartment had two bedrooms. Our dining area had a small box for a window air conditioner. We couldn't afford one, so the box in the wall was always empty, with slats across the opening so that air could flow in and out of the boxed area. One spring, a tiny bird made its way into the box. We heard some rustling, so my dad opened the screws to see what was inside. We gently and quietly peeped in through the tiny screw hole. To our surprise, we saw a bird busily building a nest. After a few weeks, we saw some eggs in the nest. Then we had small chicks chirping inside the air conditioner box. It was an amazing sight. Every morning, we would look inside the hole, and we'd look again when we returned home from school. The cycle of life was played out of in front of our eyes.

The Spirit is revealed as one who shelters those in difficulty (Psalm 17:8) or lifts up the enslaved on her great wings (Exodus 19:4), like a bird protecting her chicks. She is depicted as a woman knitting together new life (Psalm 139:13), as a midwife, (Psalm 22:9–10), and as a woman scrubbing away at bloody stains (Isaiah 4:4).[5]

---

Such beautiful feminine imagery for the Spirit, and then Isaiah goes and makes me have visions of the Spirit as Lady Macbeth.

**THE ACOLYTE**

---

In the New Testament, the Spirit is tied to the ministry and resurrection of Jesus Christ and the growth of the disciples. During Jesus' baptism, the Spirit descends upon him in the form of a dove (Luke 3:22), the emblem of Aphrodite, goddess of love in Greek mythology. This feminine imagery of the Spirit complements the masculine understandings of the Divine. Doves were favored and honored in many times and places, and they often enjoyed cultic protection, with towers erected for them and a steady supply of food provided. In France, dovecotes were a privilege of the wealthy, and only those with social status could build one. In Christian art, the figure of the dove is linked with the Holy Spirit in a backdrop of divine female power.

**THE DEACON**

I wonder if the ancients ever imagined that contemporary Christian music would co-opt the dove and use it to name their annual award show? I'm going to guess no.

How might we imagine a feminine Trinity? It would revolutionize Christianity as a religion that exemplifies and employs gender justice. It would bring my children hope for a new world without violence and oppression against women. Women would no longer be viewed or treated as second-class citizens. Think of all the possibilities with a feminine Trinity.

Johnson recognizes feminine metaphors about the Spirit in John's account of Jesus speaking to Nicodemus. Jesus says a person must be born anew to enter the reign of God. Nicodemus asks how anyone can be born after having grown old. Jesus replies, "No one can enter the reign of God without being born of water and the Spirit. What is born of the flesh is flesh, and what is born of the Spirit is spirit" (John 3:5–6). God's Spirit is here likened to a woman bringing forth new life through childbirth, so that those who believe are truly born of God.

All of humankind depends on women's special ability to give birth. The Spirit, too, is responsible for the birth of new life. Johnson insists that the feminine Spirit is in the world and is active. The Spirit calls out, sanctifies, and animates the church. The Spirit wipes away the debt of sin and raises people from being dead to grace. The Spirit is a life giver.

Another feminine imagery that we can find in the scriptures is "Sophia," which is Greek feminine word for wisdom used in the New Testament. Feminist theologian Elizabeth A. Johnson uses the term "Spirit-Sophia" to convey the understanding that the Spirit is feminine and is associated with Jesus.[6] Spirit-Sophia is the divine person who opens the divine mystery into Jesus-Sophia and Mother-Sophia. Spirit-Sophia accompanies human beings to encounter the Trinitarian mystery. Spirit-Sophia is feminine, opening the imagination to divine imagery. In the past, male theologians' assumption that the Spirit is masculine shaped centuries of Christian thought, as if feminine imagery would be heretical. We can now see new ways of imagining the divine.

**THE BISHOP**

Yes! These feminine images are needed now more than ever. May the Spirit birth in us all a newfound appreciation for the nurturing and motherly God of grace.

In the Jewish tradition, the Spirit of God came to be spoken of, especially in the Talmud, as the female symbol called the Shekinah. This term is from the Hebrew verb *shakhan*, "to dwell," meaning the one who dwells, the divine presence among the people. The rabbis would say that the Shekinah descended to show God's presence in the Holy of Holies. They also said, "If two sit together and the words of the Law [are spoken] between them, the *Shekinah* rests between them."[7] It was a way to talk about the presence of God in their midst.

As children, when we were sad or afraid, the safest place in the world was in our mother's arms. When we imagined that the world was against us, coming to our mother's lap was the best feeling in the world—coming to dwell in our mother's peace, comfort, and love. In the Shekinah, God's elusive, powerful presence comes to light as a female presence, manifest in the symbols of cloud, fire, or light that leads the people, accompanying them through the exodus into an exile of harsh time. God's indwelling Spirit remained with the refugee Israelites and gave them hope.

*Shekinah* means divine compassion. When the people are brought low, Shekinah lies in the dust, anguished by

human suffering. Shekinah is a term with female reso-
nance that carries forward the biblical understanding of
God's Spirit, signifying God as She Who Dwells Within.
The Spirit mothers Jesus into life, empowers him for his
mission at his baptism, and brings believers to their rebirth
out of the watery womb of the baptismal font.[8]

---

This gives me a whole
new way to embrace my
baptism. I had never
connected the water

**THE DEACON**

with the womb before. Beautiful.

---

Over time, positive feminine images of the Spirit are
transferred to the idea of the church, as it became common
to call the church "holy mother" and to envision Mary as
mother of all the faithful. The feminine Spirit/Shekinah's
capacity to manifest a divine presence and activity in female
form seemed all but forgotten.[9] Johnson sees God as a
dynamic, tripersonal mystery of love and overflowing life.
The core that relates humans to God, to one another, and to
divine creation comes from God, the source of all life.

## Sallie McFague and the World of Panentheism

It is important to recognize our interconnectedness to one
another, other creatures, and the world. A noted feminist
ecotheologian, Sallie McFague writes that we are not separate beings but are part of an intricate web of life. We

are intertwined, and we affect each other. This is like the Asian thought that believes in the power of community, in contrast to Western Lone Ranger ideals. Asians have prioritized community or communal understanding as the key aspect of how a society grows, maintains itself, and stays together. African Ubuntu theology also emphasizes community. They say, "I am because of who we are." Being part of a community is the priority, not a focus on ourselves as individuals. Ubuntu theology forces us to recognize our shortsightedness and understand that we are all interrelated and interconnected. We do not and cannot live in isolation; we need community with others. Feminist theologians are reminding us of how our Pauline teachings have influenced our churches. We must share understanding with others, so that we can behave lovingly toward each other and for each other.

McFague uses feminine language for God. She views God as Mother and the world as God's body. In this way, she is viewed as a panentheist, and creation is God's self-expression. Panentheism considers God and the world or creation to be interrelated. The world is in God, and God is in the world. The Spirit is not so uniquely the Spirit of Jesus, according to McFague. Rather, the Spirit is the empowering Spirit. It is the breath of life and what gives us all life.

## Cynthia Moe-Lobeda and Ecotheology

Cynthia Moe-Lobeda, a feminist ecotheologian, makes a similar observation about the Spirit residing in each of us. The Spirit is our hope: it is God's Spirit living in

Panentheism is what postmodern people say so that they can explain their belief in God to a

**THE ELDER**

post-Enlightenment world. I think theism still covers it, though.

us, dwelling in our being and our lives, which will bring about change. We are not separate from the Spirit, but are one with it. This oneness with the Spirit brings healing, restores a sense of rightness, and heals our relationships.

God's Spirit is always within us, giving us life and sustaining us throughout our lives. We are the holy temples of God; this knowledge can make all the difference in how we treat ourselves, others, and nature. By recognizing God within us, we will begin to treat the world with respect, love, and compassion. In our society of multinational corporations and globalism, we need to take a deep breath, recognize the dangers, work toward justice and peace, and resist forces that broaden the power and wealth of the few over the values of the many. This is crucial to us as inhabitants of this planet and its stewards as we pass it on to our children. The Spirit has always led people to a sense of holy mystery, long before Christ was revealed and incarnated. We need to allow it to work and speak through our own lives. As our lives are transformed, others will recognize the work of the Spirit.

**THE DEACON**

The Trinity is really the preeminent corporation—in a totally benevolent and mutualistic sort of way, of course. We need more non-capitalist togetherness.

The Spirit is a constant reminder of God's presence in the world, working actively among, in, and through us. This Spirit can transform us and in turn lead us to transform the world. The Spirit is immanent, willful, and moving—not remote, fixed, and unchanging. The Spirit can sweep through the earth and bring about a new life.

We are habitations of the God who inhabits all created things, not only the human ones. Luther insisted that God and Christ are present not only in us but in all created things. God is present in our world as we bear witness of God. The mystery of creation is that God dwells within it and within us, enabling us to realize his plan for justice.

## Shamanism

My father's family was Buddhist. I remember that when I was a child in Korea, one of my aunts was a devout Buddhist who would pray most of the day and recite a sacred Buddhist passage whenever she had free time. She would faithfully visit the temple and give her offerings. I was young and curious, fascinated by her repeated prayers and the prayer beads that she held in her hand and slowly pushed through her fingers in a steady rhythmic tempo as she recited her prayers.

After we immigrated to Canada, our immediate family converted to Christianity. Our church became our life. We would go to church whenever my parents found the time to go. My parents became very conservative, evangelical Christians.

When I was young, I wasn't too sure about the religion on my mother's side. But I remember my mother trying to evangelize our families. She took my sister and me back to Korea for a visit in 1980, when I was ten and my sister was eleven. My mother was especially evangelical toward her side of the family. During that trip, she went to my grandmother's house and noticed red strings placed haphazardly in the corners of the two-room house. As soon as my mother noticed them, she got up from the floor, stood on a stool, and yanked the red strings from the corners of the room. I remember her yelling at my grandmother that she was no longer to practice Shamanism—that it was evil and that my grandmother should only pray to the Christian God. My mother said that the red strings symbolized evil and that we were a Christian family; no other religious practices or symbols should be allowed in my grandmother's house. My grandmother was a calm woman; she just said, "Okay," and never put the strings back up.

---

This story brings an all-new meaning to the term *high-strung*.

**THE DEACON**

## Chung Hyun Kyung and the Shamanistic Dance

Chung Hyun Kyung is a Korean theologian who currently teaches ecumenism at Union Theological Seminary in New York City. In 1991, when she was a young woman, she was invited to open the Seventh Assembly of the World Council of Churches (WCC) in Canberra, Australia. Chung caused quite a storm of controversy as she invited those in attendance into the spirit world of the native peoples of Australia. She came onstage dressed as a Korean shaman, along with fellow Korean and Aboriginal dancers.[10] On the stage, traditional Korean drums were playing as Chung used the shaman's dance to address the assembly theme of "Come, Holy Spirit, renew the whole creation."

Her understanding and presentation of the Spirit comes from her understanding of the Korean cultural perspective of Spirit—that the Spirit relieves the *han* of the people. *Han* is a Korean word meaning unjust suffering, resentment, bitterness, and grief.[11] People who have experienced extreme pain, grief, and injustice will have *han*, which needs to be released. A traditional Korean way to achieve this is through a shaman, who is usually a woman. Then, like a shaman priest, Chung burned a piece of paper listing the names of the spirits and wafted the burning ashes up to heaven.

Some of the assembly attendees were alarmed by Chung's presentation of the Spirit, seeing it as syncretistic and upset by her apparent mixing of Christian faith with other religious traditions. Some of them believed that you cannot have a pneumatology separate from Christology and the doctrine of the Trinity. If they are separated, these participants believed, then the spirit expressed is not the

I remember when *Han* needed to be released. That carbonite prison eventually melted away, just like my sins.

**THE DEACON**

Christian Spirit, but rather some evil spirit. In addition, many Koreans were upset that a young woman was asked to do a plenary presentation, rather than a senior pastor or theologian, as well as upset that Chung didn't distinguish the Holy Spirit from other spirits.

I can empathize with such concerns, because I have had a difficult time coming to terms with the idea that other cultures have a concept like what we have within Christianity. I was reared by parents who were biblical literalists. They revered the Bible; if a Bible was on a coffee table, nothing must be placed on top of it—not another book, a pencil, or a piece of paper—because the Bible is invested with utmost authority and power. My parents also taught me that all other religions and cultural teachings are evil.

Despite such reservations, as we consider the Spirit, we must recognize the feminist voices from around the globe. Their unique voices add richness to our ongoing dialogue on the Spirit.

What happened to the Holy Spirit in Christian theology in the 1960s when feminist theology started to emerge? Indigenous spiritualities, earth centered and feminine, were presented as an alternative to the academic

**THE ACOLYTE**

My parents taught me to question everything except them. But in the Spirit, Christianity has given me language for my more transcendent experiences.

theologies of Christianity. Ecotheology recognizes that the Spirit expresses the creative work of God. Some believe the Spirit can only work for Christians, but there has been an increasing acknowledgment that the Spirit is at work around the world in all cultures and all peoples. If this is so, then it becomes increasingly important to hear the voices from around the globe and understand how different communities view the Spirit and its presence in their lives. Theology always occurs in context, and different contexts provide different insights.

A short survey of different cultures and their understanding of the Spirit will help us understand more deeply our own understanding of the Spirit. The breath of God is conceived in different cultures and languages. In some cultures, it may not even be visualized as breath. Chung was able to evoke an Asian feminist understanding of the Spirit by tying it to an Asian cultural understanding of the Spirit that is liberated and life-giving. Her revolutionary act of empowerment at the WCC meeting in Canberra brought a new feminist perspective of the Spirit, placing Asian women thinkers in the forefront of theological discourse. As I recall this event and the aftermath, all I can think of is my mother pulling the red strings from the corners of my grandmother's rooms. It is a clear reminder of women's experience of tension in upholding spiritualities and their desire to be faithful.

## Spirit's Power

I've always liked television shows like *Isis* and *Wonder Woman*. They take me to a fantasyland where women are powerful and beautiful. Similarly, the Spirit has power to reorganize the way we see things, forming new patterns.

---

It's no surprise then that the best DC Comics movie is *Wonder Woman*. That's what happens when you let women have the power they deserve to make an awesome action-packed superhero film. Jenkins > Snyder.

**THE DEACON**

---

There are different forms of power. The power of the Spirit is "power with," a sharing of power as the Spirit vibrates and moves in us and we become collaborators with the power of the Spirit. It leads to greater accomplishments and transformations in ourselves, our society, and our world. The Spirit brings forth life-changing power as a transformative and energetic force in our lives. "Power with" encourages sharing power that affirms oneself and can also mutually affirm one another as we recognize and acknowledge the special talents of particular individuals. "Power with" is life giving, sustaining, and encouraging. There is power in the Spirit that can lead to greater accomplishments and transformations within us and in society, nature, and world. The Spirit's life-changing power becomes a transformative and energetic force in our lives. The Spirit can empower all of us, especially women, to change this world into a more just and equitable place.

# 7

# A Modern Theology of the Work of the Spirit

I have written for *Time* magazine, but I have never landed on their cover! It is my dream to be on their cover, any cover. Well, maybe not *Mad* magazine, but any magazine read by adults would be fine. It would be absolutely crazy if I ever did, because not many theologians get to be on the coveted cover of *Time* magazine. Among the few is Karl Barth. He was on the cover of the April 20, 1962, issue. His face on the cover shows just how famous he really was in the first half of the twentieth century.

Along with Barth, other modern theologians also have made a significant impact on our understanding of the Spirit. We will take a look at Barth, Jürgen Moltmann, and Sallie McFague and see how, in a globalizing world, we need to move toward a global understanding of the Spirit, which may not sound orthodox to many in the church.

**THE BISHOP**

It's about time we have a female theologian on the cover of a major publication.

## Karl Barth's Spirit for the Church

Karl Barth remains one of the most important theologians for the twenty-first century. He wrote *Church Dogmatics*, which has been a central text within systematic theology. He treats the doctrine of the church in his large volumes on the doctrine of reconciliation, and this sheds some light on his understanding of the Holy Spirit. Barth describes the Holy Spirit as the Father's love to the Son, which was expressed in God's sending of Jesus into the world. The power of the Holy Spirit is nothing less than God's power. For Barth, the revelation in Jesus Christ is sufficient. Barth regards the Holy Spirit as the one and only Spirit of Jesus Christ, which leads him.[1]

Barth tends to subordinate the Spirit to Christ, as the Spirit appears as a mode of operation of Christ in the world, rather than as a distinct person of the Trinity. Thus, Barth's pneumatology becomes locked in by his Christology, and this limitation prevents him from appreciating any study of the Spirit beyond the Christian revelation. This prevents a dialogical engagement with other world religions.

For Barth, the church is an important place for the work of the Holy Spirit. God uses us in our weakness, our sinfulness, to do Christ's work in this world as we participate in God's mission through the Holy Spirit as the Holy Spirit sends the community into the world. The church is the place of the realization of the atonement— the death of Jesus Christ. The Holy Spirit gives the gift of faith that we can be saved, and the church can respond to the work of the Holy Spirit.

---

No wonder committed Barthians haven't transitioned easily into the pluralistic discourse of the twenty-first century.

**THE DEACON**

---

Barth quotes Luther: "The Holy Spirit has called me by the Gospel, enlightened me with His gifts, sanctified and maintained me in a right faith, as He calls and gathers and enlightens the whole of Christendom, keeping it to Jesus Christ in the true and only faith."[2] The Spirit draws the community together as a community of the living Christ.

As the Spirit builds up the church, people are brought into active communion with God in Christ. They are brought into communion (*koinonia*) with each other, in the communion of saints, and live out their vocations as disciples. Our work as disciples is carried out because Christ works in us by the ongoing power of the Holy Spirit. As we worship and serve, it is the Spirit who enables all things as a witness to Jesus Christ. Here we recognize that we cannot do anything without the Spirit. The Spirit works through us.

For Barth, the Holy Spirit awakens the community, calls the community together, and constitutes the church. According to Barth, the church is a place for us to experience the Spirit, and thus it remains a valuable place for us even today.

Not everyone attending worship actually senses this experience. When my kids were younger, they couldn't wait to go to church. This was because all their friends were at church and they socialized at church. Now that they are in their teens, sometimes they ask, "Do we have to go to church today?" or will say, "Church isn't that important." They whine about it on Sunday morning, as they would rather sleep in than go to church. I have to drag them out of bed and remind them that church is important.

For those who do not find the church important, how do we then use Barth's understanding of the Spirit? Jürgen Moltmann may have a more global understanding of the Spirit that is helpful for those who have left the church or find the church as not that important.

## Jürgen Moltmann and the Spirit in All Things

Jürgen Moltmann is a leading twentieth-century Reformed German theologian who developed a pneumatology of life-giving spirit and hope. Moltmann is a professor emeritus of systematic theology at the University of Tübingen and a major scholar in modern theology. He did not grow up Christian, but his experience of being drafted into the *Luftwaffe* in World War II had an impact on his life that made him turn to Christ. As a soldier, he surrendered to a British soldier and was a prisoner of war from 1945 to 1948. He had a life-changing experience in prison when he met a group of Christians, and it was there that he found Christ.

Moltmann's suffering created a space to develop a theology of hope that infers that God suffers with humanity and promises humanity a better future through the hope of the resurrection. Moltmann observes that when one's action preserves God's creation from destruction, it becomes an action of hope. Sometimes hope is what keeps us alive when we are in the depths of agony and suffering.

Moltmann's perspective became very real to Kelly Gissendaner, a prisoner in Georgia. She was convicted of plotting the murder of her husband, Douglas Gissendaner, in 1997. In prison, she experienced a conversion to Christianity and began to minister to other women prisoners. She even enrolled in a theology studies program for prisoners, run by the consortium of Atlanta-area divinity schools. During this time, she wrote a letter to Moltmann, and they began a pen-pal relationship. They even got to meet each other when Gissendaner was finishing her theology degree in prison. Moltmann had compassion on Gissendaner and provided some hope. He wrote, "If the State of Georgia has no mercy, she has received already mercy of Heaven."[3] On September 30, 2015, despite a campaign to save Kelly Gissendaner's life, the state of Georgia carried out her execution.

As we see in the relationship between Moltmann and Gissendaner, the Spirit is compassionate. The Spirit of God will not neglect us but will be with us always. God's indwelling Spirit offers us hope, love, and peace to carry out the work of creation and salvation.

Moltmann points out that Yahweh's *ruach* is present in everything. This means that the Spirit is in all created beings. This understanding of the Spirit brings joy to our efforts to preserve this godly world. The Spirit of God dwells in creation, as there is an indwelling of God in all living things. This view is known as panentheism, the theological belief that God is in all things, as distinct from pantheism, which holds that God *is* all things.

Have you ever wondered how the Spirit can be in all things? This is a constant mystery for us. If we are created in God's image, then we can say that God is within us and in all of creation. Moltmann understands that we are one with the Spirit and we are from God and we will return to God. This oneness reminds us that we come from God, are part of God, and return to God. George Fox, founder of the Quakers, said, "There is that of God in everyone."

Moltmann writes powerfully about how the passionate love of the Trinity overflows its bounds and spills over all of creation. God's Spirit embraces all of creation. The Spirit brings us to God and pushes us to reconcile with the love of God. The power of the Spirit is so strong that it pulls us back to the creator.

God is bigger than we can imagine. However much we might want to put God in a box and present God to the church or to our friends, God fits in no box we can imagine. Christians have an unfortunate tendency to envision a god in our own image—a god who hates the LGBTQ, Muslims, foreigners, women, and so on—and present it to the community. But we cannot put God in a box and limit God. God is free and bigger than we can ever imagine. As finite beings, we have difficulty imagining the infinite. Augustine once said, "If you understand, then it is not God." His words still ring true today.

I'm only interested in a God that's outside of the box. My friends already think I'm crazy for going to church, I can't get down with judgy divinities.

**THE ACOLYTE**

I feel like all Christians who push through to this level of theology have to have gone through a Moltmann stage. His social Trinitarianism saved me from walking away from my faith after college.

**THE DEACON**

Our breath comes from within us. God's enlivening presence is this breath to us and within us. This presence does more than make us biologically alive; the Holy Spirit makes us "spiritually" alive. It inspires and strengthens us and gives us aspirations. It opens us to new truth and enables us to integrate this into our minds and lives. God's presence also assures us of divine acceptance and companionship, as it guides us and binds us to one another. We cry out for the presence of God by saying, "Come, Holy

Spirit." This does not mean we think God is located at some distance and that we are asking God to move. Rather, it expresses our hope that the universal presence of God will become more real to us. We want God to open us to the presence of the Spirit, so that we may be changed and transformed. We believe this will make us more truly alive.[4] Life is more than just the physical body. It is the spiritual as well. The Spirit awakens us to the spiritual side of our being, which can get neglected at times.

## Global Spirit

Can Christians just claim the Spirit for ourselves? Once we have something good, we want to keep it to ourselves. When I was a younger mom, I sacrificed whatever I could for my kids. Whenever someone gave us good food, I would instinctively share it with them. But then I realized that I don't have to share it with them, as they don't appreciate it as I do. So I decided to keep those treats to myself and feed myself. In similar ways, we Christians want to keep the Spirit to ourselves—that is, define it as something given only to people of our faith. But is this how it is supposed to be? We cannot limit the movement of the Spirit and wonder how we live in the world with so many cultures and religions around us. We must recognize the power of the Spirit, the movement of the Spirit, and that the Spirit is unbounded by Christianity alone. Oneness of the Spirit brings healing and makes relationships right. As the Spirit of God resides in each of us, we project that Spirit to others around us.

In my travels, I meet a lot of scholars around the globe. When I was in South Africa, the Africans told me they have a similar understanding of the Spirit as the Asians. And their understanding of the Spirit existed way before the white missionaries arrived in Africa.

---

The Spirit crosses borders and builds bridges. I wish more global leaders were

**THE BISHOP**

attuned to its movements. Maybe then we could move toward world unity.

---

The Spirit dwells among us. It exists in all things, and gives all living things energy and breath. God's Spirit is always within us, giving us life and sustaining us. We are the holy temples of God, and this knowledge can make the difference in our relationships. By recognizing that God is within us, we begin to treat ourselves, others, and nature with respect, love, and compassion. This is crucial to us as we try to live on this planet and to sustain it for our children. The Spirit has always led people to a sense of holy mystery, long before Christ was revealed and incarnated. The Spirit energizes and empowers us toward a deeper community of faith and a deeper meaning of life as sacred within all God's creation. The Spirit works miraculously in the different communities of faith to actualize the presence of God in our lives. We cannot silence the Spirit but must allow the Spirit to work and speak through our own lives. As our lives are transformed, others will clearly recognize the work of the Spirit within us.

The Spirit provides a constant reminder of God's presence in the world, working actively through us as we pursue justice. The Spirit can transform us and in turn lead us to transform the world. In the minds of many theologians and philosophers, the Spirit is immanent, willful, and moving, rather than remote, perfect, and unchanging. The Spirit as wind and breath gives us new life.

## Spirit's World

Does the Spirit belong to Christianity, or does it belong to the world? Can it even be limited to the earth? I was excited to follow US astronaut Scott Kelly's social-media posts as he spent a year in space. His pictures of the earth from the International Space Station were intriguing and both geographically and spiritually profound. His pictures reveal a different perspective of the world. One can get a view of how the earth appears so small in this vast universe. God has created all of this. If God is vast, so is God's Spirit and the Spirit's movement. To grasp the knowledge of the Spirit is beyond our comprehension. It is ludicrous to limit God's Spirit.

Can one religion—Christianity—contain the Spirit, or does it belong to everyone? When we think about our planet, the solar system, and the universe and beyond, we realize that the Spirit is larger than Christianity or even our earth-centric view of creation. We understand that the Spirit is in all of creation and moving in all of creation. The Spirit cannot be bounded by the confines of Christianity. It extends beyond the earth to all of God's creation. Thus, Christians cannot have a monopoly on the Spirit. The Spirit moves as it will and will be who it will be.

I remember reading Sagan's *Pale Blue Dot* before the turn of the century. If that kind

**THE ELDER**

of cosmic knowledge doesn't give us Christians a dose of epistemic humility, I don't know what will.

At times, Christians want to talk about the Spirit as if it belongs only to Christians. Although the Spirit is not limited by Christian language (it has existed before Christianity, even Judaism, and will exist long after), Christians often say that "the church has the Spirit" or "Christ has the Spirit" and "sends the Spirit to the world." This language binds the Spirit to Christ and in turn to Christianity. But as we view the world and the universe, a christologically confined Spirit is problematic. Spirit manifests itself in the world as a whole.

This way of viewing the Spirit can help us gain a different understanding of the Holy Spirit and the Spirit within us, which in turn informs our global understanding that the Holy Spirit is the Christian vision of a universal human perception. The Spirit is Godlike, and no one community can limit its nature. It is free to move as it wishes in the world. The gift of life and the struggle for the equality of life are sustained by the Spirit's power. This cannot be contained in the church or within Christianity. The Spirit manifests itself in the world. The

Spirit proceeds from the whole world as it manifests itself in nature.[5]

---

**THE DEACON**

This distinction is so crucial for Christians to understand in moving forward. Too many trump-card theologians get coercive, when the Spirit is universal and uncontainable.

---

We need to be aware of the Spirit's presence and make room for its participation, allowing it to work within us. Whenever we welcome and embrace the Spirit within our lives, we draw nearer to God. As ecofeminist theologian Sallie McFague reminds us, God is in all things because all things are in God. God is ubiquitous; God is wherever creation is.[6] God is all around us. The Spirit empowers us and possesses us to act, taking care of each other and of creation. It implores us to deepen our knowledge of God and challenges us to search the world for more ways of speaking about the divine.

Christianity has tried to legislate its version of the Spirit too long, embedded in the spread of Christianity by European colonization. Western Christianity was coloniz- ing the world and imposed our sense of the Spirit to the colonized. When Christianity plays its imperialistic role, it tends to view itself as superior to belief systems where the culture is oral, not written. Thus, the primitive stranger becomes the Other, a stranger not like us and less worthy than us. But if we listen to all the different voices of the Spirit, we find an "open space" wherein we encounter the other in his or her full dignity and uniqueness.

The Christian doctrine of the Spirit's freedom is capable of opening dialogue. As the Spirit moves in our lives and gives us breath, life, and sustenance, we become open to all the movements of the Spirit in all parts of the world, traditions, cultures, and religions. This is the movement of the Spirit that no one person, doctrine, or church can stop.

## One World and One Spirit

My parents taught me to believe only in Jesus and that Christianity is the true religion. They taught me that other religions were false and that I should not try to study them or consider them. So it was with much trepidation during my doctoral work that I took a world religions class with Dr. Ovey Mohammed. He introduced world religions as something from which we should all learn and grow. He exorcised the fear from me, enabling me to learn and be challenged by other religions.

Thus, in my doctoral studies, I examined the concept and figure of wisdom within Buddhism, Confucianism, and Shamanism. I studied other world religions and began to see the similarities and differences. I grew enough to be able to write my first book, *The Grace of Sophia*, a work comparing Christian wisdom with other religious understandings of wisdom. It led me to examine the questions of exclusiveness, inclusiveness, and pluralism—issues with which I continue to struggle.

I reconciled my struggles with the knowledge that I am finite, trying to understand the infinite, and I cannot

**THE BISHOP**

The struggle for collective liberation still continues. I'm in it with you.

comprehend all the intricacies of the divine and the Spirit. But the joy comes in the struggle to gain a deeper understanding of the Spirit in light of different cultures. We are living in a global community, where more and more different cultures are discovered among our new neighbors. As ideas, concepts, and religions collide, we can study them, compare them, and learn from them.

So this has become part of my theological journey. How do we reconcile what we encounter within the world? As I study and learn about the Spirit, I come across similar terms in different parts of the world. Holy Spirit is *Ruach Ha Kodesh* in Hebrew and *Spiritus Sancti* in Latin. These terms are similar to the Spirit. Furthermore, a similar idea is expressed in the holy scripture of Islam, the Qur'an. The words *nafas*, meaning Allah's own breath, and *ruh*, meaning Allah's own soul, are used to mean the human breath and human soul—confirming the idea that we originate from Allah and in the end will return to Allah. Breath is essential for all living things. In the Eastern tradition, breath is understood as an essential component for the well-being of the mind, body, and spirit. Breath is part of the healing process for physical disease and emotional pain. Importantly, breath is a divine energy that regulates human emotions and the equilibrium of the body.[7] It is what makes us human and connects us to the divine.

We who are finite beings cannot limit God's presence and expression in God's creation. We should not discard or suppress preexisting experiences of the wondrous Spirit because they are not expressed with the same words and ideas found in our Judeo-Christian Scriptures or, even worse, in our Latin theologies. New understandings of a cosmic Spirit open our imagination, removing the limits we place on our worldview. This opening can provoke fascinating explorations of the infinite God we worship. It will reinstate the mysterious aspect of the Divine and open possibilities of creativity, love, and wonder. The understanding of Spirit is all that and more. New expressions, new music, new art, and new rituals open wide our view to a deeper understanding of the Trinity in Christianity and of analogous tenets in other faiths.

This liberating work of the Spirit stands in dramatic contrast to the usual way we do religion: We try to confine the infinite God to a neatly decorated box, defined by our biases, ideas, concepts, and understandings. Even worse, we imagine that we have other boxes where God has no place. We feel we know all that we need to know about God. But humanity needs to widen its understanding of God, through new ways of experiencing the Spirit. This will challenge our preconceptions, requiring us to get out of our comfortable chairs and explore the discomfort we experience about an ever-reforming image of the Creator and sustainer of all that is, was, or ever will be.

We need to recognize that it is difficult for a religion to be culturally neutral—that is, free of characteristics unique to one culture or another. As the Hebrews wandered in the desert, they recognized that their practices and understanding of Yahweh were influenced by their neighbors. For example, the Hebrews' view of wisdom was influenced by the Egyptian concept of Isis, as similarities in writing styles, actions and attributes are present in biblical and Egyptian texts.[8] Nobody lives in a vacuum, and everyone is influenced by cultures, practices, philosophy, and religious traditions of their neighbors. Therefore, we need to reexamine the historical roots and cultures that led to the formulations of doctrines—especially Eurocentric theology, because of its connection to imperial domination. Early monarchs and popes sent missionaries to northern Europe to convert the barbarian races, and in the Age of Exploration, Jesuit missionaries were sent with the conquistadores to the New World. Up to the present, Catholics and Protestants have sent missionaries to frontiers in the Americas, Africa, Australia, and Oceania (Pacific Islands). Christian denominations proselytize the colonial world as if that were the only spiritual alternative. As a result, Christian doctrine and globalization are related. The problems of one are inseparable from the problems of the other.

**THE DEACON**

Thank God for Pope Francis. I know he's not perfect, but at least he got the repudiation of the Doctrine of Discovery right! Now to move on to repudiating the patriarchy.

The globalization of European culture has exported a European way of understanding God and God's Spirit to wherever the English, the Spanish, the French, the Dutch, and the Germans have (literally) set up shop. It is so powerful that many people around the world believe that God really is a white male. In that worldview, anything different from a white Mediterranean man becomes an aberration of our understanding of Jesus and of God. However, this ignores the traditions, spirituality, and cultures of peoples around the globe. It has preached to populations that their spirituality and religious traditions are "wrong." It has maligned as primitive, animistic, or savage spirituality that differs from European beliefs. This theological colonization needs to be questioned and exorcized.

Christianity is shrinking in Europe and North America.[9] As it moves to the Global South, the importance of hearing nonwhite voices and having those voices mixed into white Christianity is increasing. It is now time to seek out and embrace a global understanding, a theology of theologies. By this, I mean that we cannot ignore what the rest of the world is thinking about God without the resurrected Christ and with an immanent rather than transcendent Holy Spirit. Today we need to engage in conversation with worldwide partners to begin the process of discerning an ecumenical understanding of the Spirit. We need to push the confining boundaries that have been too restrictive to allow the Spirit to breathe, move, and blow as it wishes.

Some may think this move will jeopardize Christianity. Others think it will alter Christianity. Still others believe that it will allow bad spirits to move in and make us confused. This is fear of the unknown and a symptom of an insecure faith. Fear enslaves us. The task of the Spirit is to free us from fear. Christianity always involved a mixing of different cultural and religious understandings until the Reformation's search for doctrinal purity led to secessionism in place of syncretism. Even before Christianity, the Hebrew people who roamed around the desert recognized some borrowing, and the Hebrew understanding of wisdom had some influence from the Egyptian concept of Isis.[10]

---

**THE ELDER**

A theology of theologies sounds like a move for millennials to make. Call me stuck in my ways, but I'll keep it traditional Christian, so the only jeopardizing I do is with Alex Trebek.

---

Gaining this kind of awareness can be challenging, interesting, and even enriching. In one of my theology classes, I had some students who were Pentecostal, Presbyterian, Lutheran, or Unitarian. They all had some differences in values and beliefs. However, some who confessed to a less "pure" Christianity, to the dismay of other students, never failed to remind me of the pagan practices and influence within Christianity. As we examine the traditions of Christmas and Easter, we see the pagan sources and how they changed. We just need to remind ourselves of the irony that now and then, especially in the earliest days, missionaries did adopt pagan customs into the "unofficial" canon of seasonal celebrations.

It is through differences between Christian and non-Christian traditions that we begin to enrich our own way of understanding God. Contemplation, imagination, and discernment are needed to move us toward an understanding of the kaleidoscopic cultures of this planet. When we engage in contemplation, we can see how the Spirit acts. When we are focused on imagination, we can see how the Spirit acts. We cannot limit the Spirit's mediums. The Spirit will be where the Spirit will be. Cultures, customs, and social identity inform and transform theology. Therefore, we open ourselves to indigenous forms of spirituality that speak to the people and encourage them to transform the world.

## Modern Times and the Spirit

When we look at figures like Dr. Martin Luther King Jr. and Mother Teresa, we are amazed at their spiritual achievements despite the limitations, difficulties, and challenges they faced. Dr. King lived during a time of racial oppression in the United States, when blacks did not have the right to vote and racism led to their being arrested illegally and even lynched. Dr. King could advance the civil rights movement based on his Christian beliefs. He led the 1955 Montgomery bus boycott and organized nonviolent protests in Birmingham, Alabama, and other locations. Dr. King also led the March on Washington in 1963, when he delivered the "I Have a Dream" speech. He could achieve strides in the civil rights movement that could not have been achieved without his diligence, vision, and faith in the Spirit.

Mother Teresa was born in Macedonia and became religious. In India, she founded the Missionaries of Charity, a religious congregation that runs hospices, homes for people with HIV/AIDS and leprosy. She founded soup kitchens, health clinics, counseling programs, orphanages, and schools. She served the poorest of the poor in Calcutta. She did not have much support in the beginning, but as others saw the movement of the Spirit in her, they wanted to join the movement. When I was a seminary student, I had the opportunity to visit her compound in Calcutta. Sisters and volunteers came from all parts of the world to help in this ministry.

While Dr. King talked about the power of the Holy Spirit and that it moves us to act, Mother Teresa talked about the presence of the Spirit. In fact, both understood the presence of the Spirit. The Spirit moved and stirred Dr. King's heart to do what many others did not have the courage to do. His response to the inequality imposed on blacks was a faithful commitment to work for justice. In the same way, the Spirit informs all of us to work for justice. There is still much work to be done for justice among peoples by our love of those alive now, including those who are our children. The Spirit's power for peace moves us to work for change.

The Spirit is the mover and shaker of our lives. It is the light of the Spirit that will motivate us to work for change in our world. It is the movement of the Spirit that will transform our inner being and beliefs to make a difference in the world. With the transformative power of the Spirit, we can achieve great things.

If Dr. King and Mother Teresa were down with the Spirit, count me in. I just need to think of a way to explain it to my secular friends.

**THE ACOLYTE**

As Christians, we cannot limit our thinking to a sparse, transcendental notion of the Spirit. We need to be able to live with the Spirit, through the Spirit, and by the Spirit in order to experience the inner transformation that will help us transform the world. We need to allow the Spirit to move us to change injustices where we find them.

# And Here's Something Else to Consider: The Spirit as Chi

The coming of the Spirit is the church's birth story. Like every good birth story, it is unique. We learned it, we interpreted it, we claimed it, and we shared it.

I want to end this book by telling the story of the Spirit in the church. I want to celebrate it and wrestle with it. I want to invite you into the memories I have with it, like the time it shook me to the core in high school.

But I also want to let you in on a secret. Our story of the Spirit isn't the only one that exists. In fact, every culture holds onto unfamiliar stories. But all are important if we want to grasp at just what, who, and how the Spirit is *the* Spirit in the world.

Here's the thing about birth stories—they are nothing like what you see on TV. They aren't effortless or painless. And you don't forget the pain.

## Giving Birth to a Chi

When I was pregnant with my first child, my husband and I decided not to find out ahead of time whether it was a boy or a girl. We wanted it to be a surprise. But everyone who saw me and my growing belly thought I was going to give birth to a son. Friends, family, and strangers approached me and said, "That is definitely a boy!" Not a single one thought otherwise. My friends and family threw me three baby showers. At each shower, guests brought boy clothes, boy toys, and boy's accessories.

On the evening that my labor began, I became very nervous around 11:00 p.m., just as I was getting ready for bed. The pain continued all through the night, and when it became regular around five in the morning, I decided it was time. I woke up, and my very, *very* sleepy husband and I drove to the hospital, full of anxiety.

We checked in at the hospital around 6:00 a.m., and my doctor came into the room soon after. He examined me and said I probably wouldn't give birth until the evening. "What?!" I exclaimed. There was no way I was going to be in labor all day. I thought to myself, "This is wrong; this trained medical doctor who went to school for ten years is just wrong. I am going to have my baby by noon."

Later that morning, my mother-in-law called the hospital room and told my husband that since I was going to have a boy, I'd better have it at night. I had no idea what she was talking about, as I was in and out of consciousness as my labor progressed. All day, I wasn't sure whether I was really in labor and about to give birth, or was being delirious. I imagined myself being cooked alive in the hospital whirlpool, where I sought refuge from my pain. The hot water overheated my exhausted body, causing more pain; in and out of awareness I went. All that kept going through my head was that I needed to get my baby out of me. It was my first labor, and I did not want it to be a long one. Impatiently, I said to myself, "This doctor has no idea what he is talking about, and I don't need to listen to my mother-in-law, I just need to give birth as soon as possible. I need to deliver a new life into this dangerous and complex world, hopefully by noon."

Noon came and went, and still no baby. In the afternoon, my older sister came to the hospital and cheerfully announced that her father-in-law had checked the "books" in Korea, an Asian astrology, and forecast that I was due to have a boy. At this point, I didn't care about the gender of the baby; I just wanted it out of me. But those closest to me were rooting for me to have a boy, and to have it at night to make that fact certain.

After an agonizing day of labor pains, at 9:00 p.m., my doctor came in again, examined me, and said I was ready to give birth. He (finally) asked me to start pushing.

When you watch birthing shows on television, pushing looks so easy, like you groan a bit, with slight dampness glistening on your skin, and the baby just pops out miraculously. But if you have a baby the size of a watermelon inside of you, no matter how hard you push, it feels like nothing you can do will make it budge. After a while, I felt that it was a useless effort, but the nurses kept encouraging me to push. So I faked it to make them happy; I didn't have the energy or the determination to push. I was tired and, weirdly enough, ready to move on and take a break.

---

**THE BISHOP**

#RealTalk. The old adage "It's easier to give birth than to raise the dead" was likely *not* written by a woman.

---

So it seemed like a mystery to me when my doctor said that the baby's head was coming out. He yelled, "The baby's got a lot of hair!" My heart began racing again, and I instinctively started to push so hard that I believed every vein in my body would rupture. After I pushed for what seemed like an eternity and screamed so much that my husband started to become fearful of my very well-being, at 9:23 p.m., my baby entered the world.

It was indeed a baby boy! Everyone was so happy and excited. I have shared my birth story with my children many times, and they love it; they know it better than I do by now. They recount it just to make me relive the moment when I may or may not have threatened all the medical staff in my birthing room. They never let me gloss over the details or forget my conflicted emotions while navigating my family's expectations, or even my inability to control what was happening. This attention to events—not only for personal narratives, but also for that which shapes what is beyond us—is why storytelling must be preserved.

## Context Matters

When we do theology, we can't ignore our personal and communal experiences. Our context, our history, and our knowledge all come into play to help us understand the divine. This is true of my giving birth to my first child, in that it connected me to my Asian roots in many ways. It didn't matter whether my son was born in Canada, South America, Africa, or Australia; he was going to come out Asian. Asianness is part of everything he is—his skin, nose, eyes, and hair. It is in his DNA. His Asianness cannot be separated from his identity. I apply this firsthand knowledge of my son to the theological knowledge that he is made in the image of our Creator God, through the same Spirit as you and me. That tells me we cannot accept a theology that excludes voices from around the globe. From my perspective, we need to include Asian thought, culture, and practice in our theological investigations. To understand the Spirit as Asians and Asian Americans, we need to search our history and culture for a deeper insight.

Here's the thing. What we often call "theology proper" is really theology as it was developed in Europe and America after the Reformation, within university traditions such as the Tübingen School and the neo-orthodoxy of Karl Barth. And my point is not that this theology is bad; in fact, I believe it is a faithful expression of the Spirit coming organically out of those cultures, peoples, and time. It's just that when the language and concepts from this perspective are the only ones we recognize as theology, we forget the meaning of the many-tongued eruption that was Pentecost.

**THE DEACON**

I'd imagine it was pretty hard to forget the many-tongued eruption for those who experienced it.

As you have seen in the book, I speak about theology as an Asian Presbyterian feminist theologian (I know, it's long) who has had to rediscover much of my native tongue. This rediscovery has enriched my faith and taught me how powerful our theology can be when it is truly a theology from all the peoples. I tell my delivery story because I hope it will give insight into my spirit, my Chi. Through the story, we might catch sight of that fiery, passionate Pentecostal Spirit buried so long ago.

*Chi* is an Asian word that means spirit. It has historical and religious significance in various Asian cultures and societies. If you have ever attended a tae kwon do, tai chi, or aikido class, you will recognize the word *Chi* or *ki*. These three martial arts can harness the intangible energy called Chi. Practicing them creates not only more energy but also greater health and life within oneself. This line of thinking can be extended into our popular culture. For example, *Star Wars* fans may find it easier to relate Chi to the Force, the powerful metaphysical flow of energy in the *Star Wars* universe. The concept of the Force derives from Chi quite consciously through creator and director George Lucas and has entered our culture with such lines as "May the Force be with you." Much like Chi, the Force is understood to surround and penetrate us. Practitioners of the healing art of Reiki also understand this idea of a life force energy in all of us. To practice Reiki is to harness this energy and spirit in healing oneself or another person. The energy is given by the "laying on hands"—not so different from the Christian practice of laying on hands for healing, prayer, and ordination.

---

If Episodes I to III are any indicator, I'm pretty sure the Chi left Lucas a long time ago. I think it latched on to J. J. Abrams, though.

**THE DEACON**

---

In this way, Chi is part of the everyday lives of Asian people, just as it is part of their everyday vernacular. People will greet one another, try to gauge each other's Chi level, complement each other's good Chi, and attribute their sickness or low energy to "low levels of Chi." Chi is an energy that brings wholeness, health, and vitality. Chi gives life, and without it, there is no life.

---

The reductive explanation of Force sensitivity to one's midichlorian count was totally disenchanting.

**THE BISHOP**

A deeper study of Chi may help us appreciate the meaning of Spirit for Asians and Asian Americans. Chi helps broaden our pneumatology (theology of the Holy Spirit) and enriches our dialogue and understanding of Spirit for all people around the globe.

## A Pneumatology of Chi

Who or what is the Holy Spirit? I have studied and written about it for many years, yet I find that I am still trying to work it out. I'm secretly hoping that writing this book will help me articulate it. One thing I believe is that the Spirit exists within all of us.

But if the Holy Spirit dwells in us, how do we realize that Spirit? Wise ones tell us to center ourselves, to allow the Spirit or the Chi to enter into our lives. As we allow Spirit/Chi to indwell us, it will push out any unnecessary things and make our lives energetic, life-giving, and strong. That's the promise.

As a Korean Canadian/American Christian theologian, I'm struck by the similarity of Chi and the Holy Spirit. Chi is vital energy and the essence of the material body. Chi has its origin rooted in God and is the life force of living creatures. Human beings live through the breath of Chi, which penetrates our entire bodies. Healing is associated with the circulation of Chi: not only is breath the power that sustains and restores life, it also is the power that changes, transforms, and heals all living things.[1] Chi heals our mental and spiritual entities, as well as our physical bodies. All these concepts emanate from the life-giving Spirit that is in all things and is the Spirit that God has provided us. It is the spiritual energy and form that inhabits all of us. It is a dynamic, living, and vital force, a mysterious bridge between God and human-ity.[2] Chi is the connector that draws us to the Divine.

The Old Testament *ruach*, the New Testament *pneuma*, and Chi encompass the concept of wind, which symbolizes a powerful force in nature, and breath, which symbolizes the power of life in the living. *Ruach* is part of the creation story when God breathes into Adam and gives him life (Genesis 2:7). It is the life-giving Spirit that gives life and new energy to the dry bones (Ezekiel 37). In Eastern cultures, there is no life without Chi. Similarly in Western cultures, nothing can live without the enlivening Spirit; the two concepts overlap.

In an increasingly multireligious, multilingual, and multicultural world, it is increasingly important to recognize the differences and similarities among people, cultures, and religions. The world's religions do not generate many separate spirits, but rather various names and understandings for the Spirit. Chi reminds us that God is always within us. We are the holy temples of God, and our knowledge can make all the difference in how we treat ourselves, others, and nature.

**THE BISHOP**

Bringing this kind of unity of Spirit into perspective reminds us of our global connection with all planetary life. This Spirit sustains us all as we are temples in that larger temple that is our cosmic and sacred space.

## Tigers Should Be Born at Night

A few years after my son's birth, I found out why my mother-in-law wanted me to give birth at night, rather than in the daytime. My first child was born in the year of the Tiger in the Chinese calendar, which is widely used by Koreans. In the year of the Tiger, it is said that a boy should be born at night, and a girl in the daytime. Tigers roam and hunt at night and sleep in the day. Therefore, if a boy is born at night, then the boy will become strong, fearless, and full of energy, while a girl born in the daytime will be meek, quiet, and subservient, in keeping with the traditional, patriarchal understanding of gender roles. In Asia, many do not want a strong-willed and outspoken girl or a weak, inactive boy.

Though I don't believe in Chinese calendar traditions, they are part of my culture. It is important for me to recognize how the ingredients of my culture—my upbringing, my family, and my Asian American community—help to define me.

The Chinese calendar and its legend of the year of the Tiger are based on folklore and a long history of storytelling, but this much is true: my firstborn son is physically, mentally, and psychologically strong. When my family had the flu, he never got it. It cycled through everyone else twice, but my son never succumbed. I never had to take him to a doctor, while it seemed that my daughter's second home was the doctor's office. During his last year of high school, my son is the captain of the soccer team and a member of the lacrosse and the track and field teams. His Chi is very powerful. He is so strong that when I am near him, I can feel physically and emotionally drained (sorry, Theo).

In English translations of Chinese philosophy, *Chi* translates as breath. The Asian understanding of breath is more physical than the metaphysical *ruach* of Genesis. The life-giving Chi becomes spiritual when human beings "have joined with the Creator as men to wander in the single breath of heaven and earth."[3] Human beings live and die with the breath of life. While the Asian notion of breath has some similarities to the Hebrew and Greek concepts, the Asian sense is subtler yet more tactile. Chi sustains and restores life. Chi is the spiritual energy and form that inhabits all of us. Chi becomes a mysterious bridge between God and humanity,[4] the connector that draws us together closer to the Divine.

I understand the Spirit's dwelling in us by the Chi that my son embodies. When people meet both my son and me, they see my son's Chi as stronger than mine, so strong that it overshadows my own. His strong Chi diminishes my weak Chi. Friends have persuaded me to find ways of raising my Chi so I can remain strong and function more effectively. They suggest Chinese medicine, tai chi, breathing techniques, meditation, and being mindful of the Spirit.

Chi embodies and dwells within us. This is a powerful aspect of the Spirit that gets lost or diminished in Eurocentric theology. This beautiful Asian cultural recognition of Chi brings us back to the *ruach* that dwelt on the land, where people experienced it as wind and breath. It was within them, and it gave them life. It was the powerful wind that separated the Red Sea as they fled Egypt. The wind gave them life.

In the Christian tradition, Chi reminds us of the Pentecost when the Spirit came in among the gathered

**THE DEACON**

The Chi split the sea?!
Mind = blown.

worshippers with tongues of fire upon them all (Acts 2). The people were filled with the Holy Spirit. Chi shows and reminds us that Spirit embodies us.

Although Chi and its underlying concepts are more complex than I know, this experience of birthing and raising children has clearly shown me that it is part of the daily lives of Asians. It is the lens through which we see the world, make sense of relationships, judge the character of another person, and reveal whether you are well or not. If you are not well, people will try to make you feel better by helping to build up your Chi. For Asians, Chi is the spirit of life and the key to wholeness.

## Low-Chi Syndrome

To be honest, my son has an energy level that never shuts down. When he was a young kid, he couldn't stay seated for long periods. He would take one bite of his dinner, then run around the whole house, and then come back and eat another bite of his meal. It was impossible to keep him seated for more than ten minutes at a time. It was a huge headache to raise him, as his Chi was unbelievably overbearing. When I met a Korean friend during one of my visits to Toronto, the first thing she said was, "Your

Chi is so low; we need to do something about it." Then she saw my son. She immediately told me, "The reason your Chi is so low is that your son's Chi is so strong. He is draining all your Chi when he is near you. We need to remedy your Chi." Her assessment is common practice among Koreans.

You can build up your Chi by trying to do something fun or something meaningful. It may involve listening to someone's hardship or difficulty. It may even involve sharing a communal meal. When Asians eat a communal meal, the food is prepared, placed in the center of the table, and shared among everyone. In a Western meal, each person will get a piece of the main dish—for example, each person will get chicken, like the breast or leg—but in a communal meal, the chicken is cut up into tiny pieces so that it can be picked up with chopsticks. In this way, if one has extra guests, there is always enough food or room around the table. It may mean that everyone around the table gets a little bit less chicken, but it also means that the meal is enjoyed with an underlying sense of inclusivity and community.

In a communal society, nobody wants to eat alone. People want to enjoy meals together. Eating communally builds up everyone's Chi. Community trumps the individual. But that also means that everyone's Chi affects everyone else's Chi. Around the table—what Western Christians might call the "communion of saints"—a meal is shared, but Chi also is shared. Those with strong Chi offer their strength to those with low Chi. It's the gift of the communal meal.

Being full of Chi is so important because it is life-giving energy. And I can fill my life with Chi not only

**THE ELDER**

This image of the communal table helps me picture Chi. Before that, all I could conjure up were my fraternity brothers. Not a pretty sight.

through communal meals but also through activities I enjoy, through physical touch, and through giving and receiving encouragement. This is how Chi works. Chi can bring healing to the soul and bring peace to the heart. It is Chi that sustains us and gives us everlasting life.

To Western Christian readers, all this talk of Chi may sound irrelevant, or it may sound vaguely familiar. I'm trying to make a connection between an Eastern concept and a Western one, between Chi and the Holy Spirit. This means we must talk about what these concepts mean when we confront suffering and the issue of theodicy.

## Han

The Korean word *han* is difficult to translate into English. Two of the best translations are "unjust suffering" and "piercing of the heart." *Han* is immense pain and suffering perpetuated by an individual, a group, or a situation. *Han* tries to express the painful tearing apart of one's heart due to injustices. There is a lot of suffering in the world. *Han* is not about superficial problems, such as "I still have the iPhone 4" or "I got a speeding ticket." Rather, it is trying to describe an unjust suffering that comes from unjust political systems[5] and social systems.

We all suffer. On a hot day, with no place cool to retreat, we suffer from the heat. Likewise, on a cold day, when we don't have a heater to warm us, we suffer. We skip a meal, and we feel hungry—we suffer. There is suffering all the time. We can, and do, speak about suffering in many daily situations.

This is not what the word *han* is trying to capture. Painful experiences are common, but there is also "unjust suffering" that is inflicted on others to the advantage of someone else, with no regard for the fate of those who lose life, limb, family, goods, and property. In a modern context, we see this happen frequently when women are sexually assaulted. It happens when one person inflicts injury on another. This is the traumatic violation of one's body, spirit, and soul. When someone or something pierces our heart so that we are overcome with extreme grief and sorrow, with psychic, spiritual, and physical pain, this is *han*.

---

It doesn't sound like I should try and deal with my *han* solo.

**THE DEACON**

---

Systems such as racism, sexism, and colonialism that separate people into castes create *han*. Institutionalized practices of prejudice inflict unjust suffering upon people based only on differences in class and power. Some of the worst cases were the Shoah genocide by the Nazis, slavery in the American South, and the treatment of Chinese by Japanese invaders in Nanking. They are painful experiences that break people and tear them apart. They cause tremendous pain within the hearts of individuals and within the collective hearts of the people. As a nation, Korea carries a significant amount of *han* endured as a nation that was frequently invaded in its recent history.

One must remember that *han* can be a collective experience or an individual experience. A country or a community of people can suffer from *han* as people are colonized and subjugated. A deep collective feeling of a loss of one's identity and one's social and historical heritage can occur. Losing one's identity can be painful, since one's sense of heritage and belonging to the land can be terminally lost.

Therefore, it is important to understand the complex process of the loss of identity that occurs when one country invades, conquers, and colonizes another. Koreans have experienced several instances of occupation and annexation. The most recent occurred from 1910 to 1945, when Japan colonized Korea. Separated by a narrow body of water, Korea and Japan have had a complicated relationship through the years. Beginning in 1876, Japan inserted itself into the affairs of Korea, exercising growing influence and seeking greater control. The process culminated in 1910, when Japan formally annexed Korea. The Japanese ruled Korea until World War II ended in 1945.

Korea had its sense of history, identity, and culture taken from it by the occupying Japanese, who when the Second Sino-Japanese war began in 1937, virtually made Korean culture illegal. During the Japanese annexation, many people were imprisoned and killed. Many young Korean women and girls were taken as "comfort women" to work as sex slaves for Japanese soldiers throughout Asia. They were raped repeatedly, sometimes by as many as fifty to seventy different men in one night. Many of these women died. The women who survived lived with *han* for the rest of their lives. Each of the women suffered profound physical and psychological trauma. These deep traumas left *han*, which drove some women to suicide or severe depression. This unjust suffering arose out of sexism, colonialism, and patriarchy that make it acceptable to exploit the female race.

## Spirit Releases *Han*

*Han* is dangerous to carry for long periods of time, either for individuals or for a nation. It was understood that if *han* is not released in a positive way, it can kill or bring other disasters into one's life. It is important to our personal health and the health of those around us to release our *han*. *Han* needs to be set free for people to finally heal and move on to a more peaceful way of living.

---

It seems that America is only just now waking up to its *han*. Lord, have mercy, Christ, have mercy as we move toward peace.

**THE BISHOP**

---

In the past, in Korea, the shaman priest would go into a village and offer prayers, dance, and rituals to release the *han* of individuals or the community. This was an exercise necessary to keep individuals and communities healthy, spiritually strong, and positive.

If there are no means of releasing one's *han*, conditions can spiral into a tragic cycle of *han*, pain, and more *han*. This can result in people or communities seeking revenge, feeling *ressentiment* as Nietzsche used to identify a sense of hostility directed toward one's sense of frustration, or seeking methods of destruction if *han* is not released. The buildup of *han* can ultimately cause rage, uproar, and catastrophes.

Applying this to our culture, I still remember the infamous day that the twin towers of the World Trade Center came down. At that time, I was living in Toronto. I was nursing my six-month-old baby girl when I heard the radio reports. Thinking I had misheard the broadcast, I quickly turned on the television and saw every news station reporting the planes crashing into the Lower Manhattan skyscrapers. I could not believe my eyes. The images kept rolling on each news station, as the story was reported all day, and are seared into my memory to this day. I went from a dazed mom to a panic-stricken one in a matter of minutes. If a terrorist attack can occur in a city so close, what are the chances that it wouldn't happen in Toronto as well? After a couple of frantic calls to the Montessori preschool my two-year-old son was attending, I hurriedly picked him up in a panic.

*Han* may help us understand why the attack happened. The effects of empire and colonization lead colonized peoples to feel anger and resentment toward the

United States and colonizing European countries. In these difficult times, when people feel dominated and colonized by a world superpower, some desperate individuals, rather than peacefully releasing their *han*, resorted to the ugliest methods of terrorism.

This is an example of *han* not being released in a positive way. Rather than seeking positive ways of releasing their unjust suffering, they sought to kill as many "Westerners" on American and European soil as they could. The effects were disastrous and have left a painful scar on those who witnessed and experienced it.

Rather than seeking revenge or resorting to violence, how can a person or a community find positive ways to release *han*? I believe a better understanding of both Chi and the Holy Spirit can provide the tools to do this, but we must first learn to embrace these concepts together in our lives in resistance to the dominant theologies and cultural modes that have sought to eliminate their connection.

## Spirit as Chi

My challenge to Euro-Christians, Asian Christians—all Christians!—is to look to the concept of Chi to fill our understanding of the Holy Spirit. In the early pictorial language of Chi, the Chinese used a picture of a bowl of rice with steam rising. People in East Asia live on rice. It is the backbone of their cultural sustenance. It accompanies every meal. For Asians, rice is the essential item that gives life. When my grandmother was escaping with her young children during the Korean War, she had only minutes to prepare her kids to flee south. In that moment, she packed a small bag of rice, which she managed to carry in the inside of her pocket. She could use that rice to cook meals on the road for her seven small children. That bag of rice was the only thing she took from her house. The value of this grain is undeniably important, so it's not hard to imagine how important Chi is in comparison.

To Koreans, the spirit of life is Chi. The Hebrews used the term *ruach*, meaning wind, breath, and the life-giving Spirit. The New Testament writers used the Greek word *pneuma*, which also means wind, breath, and life-giving Spirit. And the German theologians in the eighteenth century used *Geist*, which means mind, spirit, and ghost. Some English translations will be "spirit/mind," which reinforces the intellectual and philosophical understanding of the spirit. Chi is as embedded in a culture as any of these other terms, but that does not make it inaccessible to non-Asians. Cross-pollinating this term with *ruach*, *pneuma*, and *Geist* will make our understanding of God's Spirit richer.

We in the West have made the Spirit too much of a philosophical notion that is to be pondered rather than lived with. The early Pentecostal experiences of the church and its people have been pushed aside, and dull church practices have become the standard practice. The awe and fear that the Hebrew people experienced of the Spirit is long forgotten, and now many of us treat the Spirit not as a living thing but rather as a concept that has faded away in the tradition of the church. Growing into a philosophical idea to be fancied by intellectuals and not a life-giving Spirit felt and experienced in our day-to-day lives—this is what we experience today. As many Asians are consciously aware of Chi and Spirit in everyday life and in one's daily existence, it is now overdue for the church to do likewise.

Maybe we should decolonialize some Michael W. Smith lyrics and say, "Go East Young Man" instead.

**THE DEACON**

That's where Chi can complement our usual understanding of Spirit, since Chi is a dynamic life force. Spirit-Chi is a living energy, not merely the third paragraph of the Nicene Creed. We need to be more conscious of the living, dwelling presence of Spirit in our midst and in our lives. How it's being connected to God is an asset. We need to accept the various languages for the Spirit as they open the door for us and strengthen our understanding of the mysterious God. We are to be creative and dynamic when we try to understand the mysterious power of God. As we recognize the power of Chi flowing in our bodies and in our lives, we can share it with others and with creation to make the world a better, more peaceful place to live in.

## Language Forms Our Thoughts

Language defines how we view the world. Our words form our thoughts. Our words also limit how we see the world. When we cannot find the right words to describe our feelings, thoughts, and experiences, we are confined to our own minds. Words matter. This is true even for things that you wouldn't imagine to have any connection to language, such as our understanding of the Spirit and God.

For example, there was my communication break-down with my youngest child during that arduous process known as toilet training—one of the greatest challenges in my life as a mother. I never looked forward to toilet training any of my kids, and this goes back to my teen years. When I was thirteen, I was babysitting a toddler who was being potty trained. It was an absolute nightmare. He would poop on the carpet, and I had to pick it up and clean the rug before his mom came home. He would also pee all over the place, a fact that I only discovered when I would step into mysterious puddles that were not there before. When I was raising my kids, I already was trau-matized from experiences of wet feet.

Parenting tip: If you're going on a long road trip, it's best that the child being toilet trained does not drink much before the trip. When my youngest was just start-ing to toilet train, we had a long trip from Pennsylvania to Toronto to visit my family. To prepare, I monitored his beverage consumption closely. But despite my cautionary efforts, about forty-five minutes into the ride, he cried from the back of the van, "I have to pee!" In the noise of the car with three kids, my husband's singing, and the blasting radio, I couldn't hear. I replied, "What?!"

He yelled back, "I have to pee!!"

I yelled back to him, "You have to be kidding me! Hold it!"

He said, "What?"

I craned my head back so fast that I loosened my neck, and I glared into his eyes. Again I said, "Hold it!!"

He replied, "Hold what?"

We all realize that language is important. Some-times we don't understand another person. We're lim-ited by our vocabulary, our life experiences, or even a noisy minivan. My son's misunderstanding of the col-loquial term *hold it* seemed funny at the time—until moments later, when he ended up *not* holding it in his pants. Memories like these show that we do want to be able to communicate our thoughts, ideas, wishes, and understandings to each other. We often try, but in some cases, our limited expressions prevent us. We become boxed in by our thoughts and understandings. Miscom-munication isn't limited to different languages, but also to people speaking the same language.

This happens in Christian theology. We're often bound to the limitations taught to us by a white, Eurocen-tric theology. We need to free ourselves from such limi-tations. We need to go beyond our thoughts and beyond our limiting English language and seek other expressions to help us articulate something as vast, as mysterious, and as infinite as the Spirit God. It may be a necessary mode of theological survival to search the world to find such expressions to help us articulate God. It is also vital that we begin to think about how we can embrace the power behind Chi and the Holy Spirit to invigorate our spiritual and communal selves.

## Commonalities between Chi and Holy Spirit

In an increasingly multireligious, multilingual, and multi-cultural world, recognizing the differences and similarities among people, cultures, and religions are essential. This is even more important with the rise of secular replacements for religious belief systems and rituals. The religions in the world do not display many spirits; rather, within them there are various names for a similar Spirit, such as Chi, *ruach, pneuma*, and *pana*.

Spirit is a universal concept, and exploring that concept can let us discover new methods of addressing, thinking about, and conceptualizing God. The first step will be to reexamine Spirit-Chi. Spirit-Chi is found within everyone. It is a source of empowerment and healing for the wounded.

Spirit-Chi is beyond mystery and conceptualization. It requires us to admit to the limitations of human understanding. We will never be able fully to comprehend the Divine. But Spirit-Chi provides us with new language and tools to address the mysterious encounters with the Holy. Within this hybrid space, our understanding of Spirit-Chi can draw us closer to God. It helps us develop a deeper understanding of the Creator of all that is, was, or ever will be.

Spirit-Chi is beyond culture, religion, and society, as it may support the ethos of people around the globe. When people recognize this, instead of being a barrier, Spirit-Chi will open doors for further dialogue, understanding, and acceptance. The more language we can use to talk about the Divine, the more we open our discourse and work toward accepting and embracing those who are different. It is crucial to understand God as Spirit-Chi and thereby break down barriers that colonialism has established. This Spirit-Chi is within us, empowering us toward emancipation and liberation.

The emancipatory aspect of Spirit-Chi is compelling. Spirit-Chi frees us from the bonds of evil that prevent us from celebrating life. It makes us stronger and builds bridges between us and our neighbors. Spirit-Chi is salvific within us and between us. It pulls humanity closer. It will sustain us and keep us aware of our interconnectedness and interreliance. As we recognize the commonality among all people, it will be easier to embrace and accept one another. Spirit-Chi embraces life and makes it whole.

It is essential that humanity recognize, welcome, and affirm the Spirit in all faiths. In a postcolonial world, this means Christianity can no longer monopolize the Spirit. God's Spirit-Chi fills us up, makes us whole, and helps build harmony and peace. It transcends problems endemic to the postcolonial world and liberates those caught in the middle. The Spirit is free to roam and be what the Spirit will be.

---

I think I have officially been liberated from my postcolonial Spirit theology. This *Chi* language is #zesty.

**THE DEACON**

---

## Chi = Holy Spirit

We like to say the Asian concept of Chi is similar to the Christian concept of the Holy Spirit, because that would make things much simpler. As the world continues to shrink and cultures, ideas, and religions collide, we can begin to recognize the similarities between groups of people. As we recognize the similarities, it draws us toward each other rather than drives us apart. In similar fashion, the power of drawing similarities between Holy Spirit and Chi will help build bridges between the East and the West. It's ideal to say *ruach*, *pneuma*, Chi, or spirit is each talking about the same Spirit of God.

Therefore, what Asia offers is a way to fill in the void created by Western pneumatology. In Christianity, especially as practiced in the West, there is a lack of awareness of the Spirit as the one who gives and maintains life as we know it. Westerners have given little priority to the recognition and activity of the Spirit within our daily lives. The East provides the tools for facilitating the union of the human and the divine to make Chi and the Holy Spirit the same. To some extent, Eastern Orthodox Christian practices share with Asia the notion of becoming more like God in Spirit.

In learning to understand Chi as the Spirit of God, we can also become empowered to fight racism and prejudice. Developing a deep, life-giving understanding of the Spirit is crucial to prevent further exploitation and hatred of each other. This emphasis on common ground in the shared Spirit of God will make a difference not only in how immigrants live in the Western world but in how we treat one another with love and respect. What I'm saying is this: if we can start to truly embrace Spirit-Chi as the Spirit of God that enlivens all of creation, we can overcome our divisions and live in harmony with one another and with the rest of God's creation. That's a bold claim, but I'm convinced of it.

---

**THE BISHOP**

I'm hopeful that a deepening of Spirit-Chi will aid us in bringing a critical harmony to our Christian pneumatology and empower us to live lives of justice and inclusion.

---

# Conclusion: It's Time for the Spirit, so Look Out

**H**aving the name Grace has been a bit quirky growing up in the church. People joked with me about saying "grace" at the table. People would introduce me as "amazing Grace," or people would have a story of an aunt named Grace to tell me. It is still interesting to live with such a name, as I feel like I need to live up to my name.

---

"Amazing Grace" is great, except for the whole "earth dissolving like snow" nonsense.

**THE ELDER**

The author should have read the end of Revelation before writing those lyrics.

---

We recognize that the good news that Jesus preached and that the Spirit embodied was grace. The Holy Spirit is

179

the gift to the world; it is grace to us. God's grace is transformative as it makes us anew. The Spirit is grace that changes and disrupts and challenges the world. We are taught to work for the reign of God through the power of the grace of the Holy Spirit. Grace is participation in the Divine as it is given to us and resides in us. Grace is about being set free as the Spirit frees us from the burden of trying to prove ourselves worthy, good, and desirable and sets us free to be ourselves. The Spirit moves within us and fills us so that the Spirit can move us.

Grace is the true work of the Holy Spirit, and we see the end results of this work. Augustine—who along with Paul is one of the biggest influences on Eurocentric understanding of the Spirit—says grace that comes from the Holy Spirit will result in "a delight in, and a love of, that supreme and unchangeable good which is God."[1] We are created to love, obey, and be with God. The reception of the Holy Spirit as gift (or grace) makes it possible for the human to fulfill the commandments of the law. Augustine surmises that this grace was hidden in the Hebrew Bible but is made known and available through the Spirit. Augustine understands the Spirit in light of the event of one's salvation, and thus the individual cannot be separated from Christ.

In all our brokenness, pain, loneliness, and suffering, God's Spirit as grace comes to us, embraces us, and strengthens us. It bears goodness to our lives. In the times of hardship, it comforts and heals our broken souls. When we have felt that God is a distant God, we now realize that God as Spirit, as Chi, as light, as wind, as vibration, and as breath is right with us and that God is an immanent

God. God Spirit is within us. We are challenged but also comforted by this.

We succumb to God's grace and live as pardoned and forgiven. We are forever in God's grace. God's grace is transformative. It holds no grudges. It forgives. It heals. It releases one's *han*. It builds bridges. It helps us understand that God is within us. We need to move forward in understanding that it is the grace within that liberates us and moves us.

In my encounters with racism and sexism, I have experienced tremendous pain. My experience of buying a dryer left me speechless and broken. I was inside Sears looking for a dryer. We had just moved to the United States and we needed a new dryer for our new house. So I went with my husband and three little kids. I was just browsing around looking when I saw a hefty white Sears salesmen along with two other salesmen walking toward my direction. They passed me and went to my little four-year-old girl and leaned over and said, "*ching chong, ching chong.*" I was floored. I couldn't believe that three adults would do that to my little girl. I glared at them, and they quickly walked away.

After all these years of experiencing racism, now my children who were born in North America have to experience it, too. The pain of racism can be a big burden. It is the *han* that can destroy people. During these heartwrenching times, it is to the Spirit that I can turn for comfort and for release of pain.

But this incident didn't leave me powerless. Grace moves us to act. It is the gift from God to do right in a broken world. Grace gave me the strength to confront the problem of racism. As a beginning, I called up Sears and had an hour-long conversation with a store manager. At the beginning of the conversation, the manager did not understand the problem I was presenting. By the end of the conversation, he apologized for the employee's actions and told me that something would be done to prevent such incidents from happening again. Sears confirmed that disciplinary actions would be taken toward their employee.

For the long term, grace is the strength for me to continue fighting against racism and sexism, which pervade our community, churches, and society. We need to fight, or it stays within our culture, society, and church, continuing to destroy people and communities. Grace is the merciful love and understanding of God, revealing to us that we are not alone. We can continue to fight the good fight.

## Surrendering to the Spirit

What does it mean to surrender to the Spirit? In our world, we want to control everything. We control the timer on our slow cooker; we set alarms to get us up at a certain time. We program our cell phones to manage our daily meetings and routines. We want to control our children (I am guilty of this), our diet, and our daily workouts (or lack of workouts). We are a society that needs to control every aspect of our lives.

---

**THE DEACON**

But *Control* is still my favorite Pedro the Lion album?

---

Once we lose a sense of control, we go a little crazy. Not only do we want to control our kids, our spouses, and our future, but in some ways, we also want to control God and the Spirit in our lives. But as described throughout this book, especially in chapter 1, the Spirit moves where it wishes, so we realize we have no control over the Spirit. The Spirit is free. Where it moves and what it does may not be what we imagined.

Having no control over the Spirit is alarming to many folks, as that means we are at the mercy of God and God's grace. Thus, rather than controlling God, we allow ourselves to be open to the movement of the Spirit at all times. We do not know where it blows. We do not know how it blows. But we do know that it blows in our world and in our lives. We need to be open and ready and sense its direction and its instruction. We need to be open to the challenges of the Spirit and allow the Spirit to work in our lives.

## My Mother's Last Fight

Life is full of good and bad surprises. Life is full of happiness, sorrows, and pains. Some of these we can control; others we cannot. When my mother was diagnosed with stage 4 lung cancer, my world collapsed. At first, there was numbness in my soul, but then anger filled my heart, as it felt like the situation was just not fair. My mom had done everything right. She never smoked, she exercised, she rarely ate meat, and she even ate all the cancer-preventing foods. So how could she be diagnosed with lung cancer at the age of sixty-three?

As my mother went through cancer treatments of both Western and Eastern medicine, our family witnessed her body slowly deteriorate. No treatment was going to cure her of her cancer as it spread. Eventually, the cancer made its way into the brain, and she had a stroke. The stroke left her immobile and mute. She became like an infant, who needed someone to bathe her, feed her, and change her. She lost all control over her life.

Doctors and psychologists tested her brain capacity and came to the conclusion that it was failing. A psychologist tested her cognitive ability with a simple matching game using pictures and words. My mother was unable to match the pictures to the words. She could not comprehend our words. She was losing control of both her body and mind.

In the last month of her life, my former minister came to visit her. I was overjoyed to see him and was thankful to him for making time to visit our family. As soon as he walked into my mom's room, tears started to roll down her face. The minister asked my sister and I to leave the room. While we waited outside, we were curious about what was happening inside the hospital room.

After about twenty-five minutes, my pastor emerged and told us they had prayed together. With tears in his eyes, he told us that my mother understood the prayer and was at peace. I was cynical, as she could not even under-stand me anymore. My pastor left us after telling us to go back into the hospital room and be with our mom.

When we entered the room, we saw her face. It was evident she had been crying a lot. Her eyes were red, her nose was red, and she had tissues scattered all over her lap and around her blankets. Then I noticed that her demeanor had changed, and I recognized a sense of genu-ine peace and serenity on her face. For the past six months, she had been fighting cancer and desperately wanted to beat it. Watching her fight cancer, it had been clear to me that she was afraid to die. She had felt no peace during the past six months.

However, in her conversation and prayer with my pastor, in the midst of her terminal illness, she had somehow come to accept her death and found peace. She surrendered to God and was able to come to terms that she would not live much longer. She had realized that the Spirit of God was within her, and she had found inner peace that showed on her face. Two weeks later, she passed away.

---

What a tragically beautiful story of grace in the midst of suffering. The way of surrender is the way of Jesus.

**THE BISHOP**

---

I know how difficult it is to surrender fully to the Spirit. It requires a lot from us, especially when we want so much control, predictability, and power over our lives. But without surrendering to the Spirit, we cannot allow the Spirit to move in our lives. Without giving control to the Spirit to control our lives, we are unable to let our hearts be moved for change. My mother surrendered to the Spirit, and the Spirit gave her a peace that no one else could offer. This grace helped her let go of the earthly things. This peaceful grace enabled her to surrender to God.

The Spirit provides peace, grace, and mercy in our lives. As the Spirit moves, it can help us transform each other and the world. As discussed in chapter 6, we need to allow the Spirit to enter our lives to help us release our *han*. Without surrendering ourselves, it is difficult to allow the Spirit to move within our lives so we may find our burdens slip away. Without the Spirit releasing this *han*, we will not find peace, serenity, or grace in our lives.

The Holy Spirit is not like the Spirit that was part of my childhood—a Spirit that frightened me and made me come to believe that Christians were all crazy people. The Spirit I experienced when I grew up had a much darker dimension. The Pentecostal revival services I witnessed as a young girl included speaking in tongues, yelling, screaming, dancing, falling over, and other terrifying behavior. But now we talk about a Spirit that is vibration, light, breath, and wind to transform our inner selves so we can do what is right and work for justice to make this world a "kin-dom of God."

---

**THE ACOLYTE**

I'm still a bit skeptical about this vibration-and-light Spirit talk, but all the transformation, justice, and kin-dom language has got me more interested than I ever thought I would be!

---

We need to hear the diverse voices around the globe to help us understand this mysterious Spirit. God is infinite, and we are finite. We attempt to understand the

mystery, but we will never fully grasp it. But as we journey together, the voices from women, Latin Americans,
Asians, Africans, LGBTQ persons, and others really open
our eyes and help us get a deeper grasp of the Spirit.

The Spirit empowers the Messiah to inaugurate a
reign of justice and peace and to create a community of
liberated life (Isaiah 11; 32; 61). The powerful Spirit of
God is present in our lives to change our hearts and bring
justice and goodness into the world. This is essential to the
well-being of the oppressed and marginalized. It doesn't
matter whether we are African or Asian, Christian or
Muslim; the Spirit comes to us. It is a global Spirit. The
Spirit is a spirit of love, power, justice, and grace.

The Spirit affects us by liberating, transforming, rec-
onciling, empowering, and assuring. That same Spirit
"gives life" (John 6:63) and liberates us from the power
of sin, death, and the law by justifying and sanctifying us.
Without the Spirit, there is no life. The Spirit is the life
giver. People are born anew of the Spirit (John 3:3, 5–6),
and this makes a difference in their lives and in turn the
world around them. The Spirit sets up the coming liberty
of the whole creation and begins the perfecting of the creation of human beings and of all things. The Spirit is powerful and empowers us to do God's work.

# Acknowledgments

**A**greeing to write a book is one matter. Writing a book is something different. The excitement dies after five pages of writing and self-doubt, disappointment, disillusionment, discouragement, and horror begins to fill one's life.

This book proved no exception.

Finishing a book takes focus, discipline, and determination. It also requires the encouragement and support of a community of friends and family. Many people helped me bring this book to the finish line.

I begin by thanking Tripp Fuller at Homebrewed Christianity, who invited me to be part of this amazing book series. Tripp is a visionary theologian who is contributing to the world of theological inquiry and conversation with his amazing podcast and with the series of which this book is a part.

I thank my editor, Tony Jones, for his phone calls in which he offered suggestions, reassurance, and editorial assistance. He provided encouragement and kept pushing the edges and boundaries of my writing abilities. He challenged not only my writing but also my theological boundaries. Tony made me a better writer and a better thinker.

I am always grateful to my research assistant Bruce Marold for his sharp editing work. His assistance is immeasurable as he patiently and consistently works beside me to help articulate and fashion my theological thoughts. My other assistants, Elizabeth Edminster, Daniel Mudd, and Joe Strife, read parts of the manuscript and I am grateful for their work. I would like to acknowledge Naomi Faith Bu, my niece who is currently in her senior year of university, who absorbed herself in the composition process of the book. Her dedicated time and freshly modern perspective gave new light to this book that I greatly commend. I am grateful to my friends, Mark Koenig, Donald McKim, Mihee Kim-Kort, Katie Mulligan, and Mido Hartman for reading parts of the book and providing valuable feedback and suggestions.

I thank my family for being kind and patient as I engaged deeply in this book. As my children, Theodore, Elisabeth, and Joshua, get older, they understand the excitement of giving birth to a new book. Thanks for your encouragement, kindness, and understanding. My daughter provided warm tea when I needed it to calm my nerves. My two boys offered back rubs for my aching shoulders that spent too many hours a day in front of a laptop.

I am thankful to my husband, Perry, who took on the extra load of housework and chauffeuring our children so I could meet the deadline for this book. My sister, Karen, and her family were supportive in so many ways to make this book a reality. I need to acknowledge my mother, who passed away from lung cancer and always taught me that faith is the most important thing in life. I am thankful to my father, who drove my sister and me to the various churches and church events described in this book. I honor my parents who established the foundation for my theological journey, exploration, and imagination.

This wonderful community of family and friends cannot be thanked deeply enough. The gratitude they inspire within me leads me to long to write theology that brings love, joy, and empowerment to all people.

# Notes

## Chapter 1

1. Jürgen Moltmann, *The Spirit of Life: A Universal Affirmation,* trans. Margaret Kohl (Minneapolis: Fortress Press, 1992), 40.

2. See Unitarian Universalist College of Social Justice, "Arizona/Mexico Border: Border Links; Sanctuary and Solidarity," http://uucsj.org/journeys/borderlinks/.

3. Plato, *Timaeus*, trans. and ed. Peter Kalkavage (Indianapolis: Hackett, 2001), loc. 1481 of 4161, Kindle. Note that the word *nomos* can mean either law or song in Greek. "Perform the song" may mean carry out the law.

4. Kenneth Sylvan Guthrie, compiler and trans., *The Pythagorean Sourcebook and Library*, ed. David Fideler (Grand Rapids: Phanes, 1988), loc. 386, Kindle.

5. Sounds may be communicated by vibrations in materials other than air. The blind can appreciate piano music by feeling the vibrations in the wood of the piano through their fingers and the low frequency percussive vibrations of drums in their feet, through the wood in the floor.

6. Wolfhart Pannenberg, *Systematic Theology*, 3 vols. (Grand Rapids: Eerdmans, 1994), 2:76–77.

7. Jürgen Moltmann, *The Source of Life* (Minneapolis: Fortress Press, 1997), 10.

## Chapter 2

1. See Friedrich Nietzsche, *The Will to Power*, trans. Walter Kaufmann and R. J. Hollingdale, ed. Walter Kaufmann (New

York: Random House, 1968), loc. 570, par. 22–23, Kindle. A strong spirit exists as an active nihilism when the strength of the existing spirit may be worn out and previous goals are no longer believed.

2. Kirsteen Kim, *The Holy Spirit in the World: A Global Conversation* (Maryknoll, NY: Orbis, 2007), 16–17.

3. Rebecca Prichard, *Sensing the Spirit: The Holy Spirit in Feminist Perspective* (Atlanta: Chalice Press, 1999), 17.

4. Jürgen Moltmann, *The Source of Life: The Holy Spirit and the Theology of Life* (Minneapolis: Fortress Press, 1997), 12.

5. Margery Post Abbott, Mary Ellen Chijioke, Pink Dandelion, and John William Oliver Jr., *Historical Dictionary of the Friends (Quakers)* (Lanham, MD: Scarecrow, 2003), 137.

## Chapter 3

1. See Bart Ehrman's several books on who wrote the various books of the Bible, such as *Forged: Writing in the Name of God—Why the Bible's Authors Are Not Who We Think They Are* (San Francisco: HarperOne, 2012). On the positive side, Paul's seven genuine letters (Romans, 1 and 2 Corinthians, Galatians, Philippians, 1 Thessalonians, and Philemon) are the only books in the New Testament for which we know the true author.

2. In Aristotle's *Metaphysics*, he describes how other schools of philosophy divide principles into dichotomies, such as "limit and unlimited, odd and even, one and plurality, right and left, male and female, resting and moving, straight and curved, light and darkness, good and bad, square and oblong." In *Metaphysics in the Basic Works of Aristotle*, ed. Richard McKeon (New York: Random House, 1941) 693–96 (book 1, part 5, par. 3).

## Chapter 4

1. Veli-Matti Kärkkäinen, *The Holy Spirit: A Guide to Christian Theology* (Louisville, KY: Westminster John Knox Press, 2012), 29

2. *NPNF*$^2$ 14:3.

3. Justin Martyr, *First Apology*, 33 (*ANF* 2:133) as cited by L. Russ Bush, *Classical Readings in Christian Apologetics, A.D. 100–1800, Parts 100–1800* (Grand Rapids: Zondervan, 1983), 20.

4. Kärkkäinen, *The Holy Spirit*, 24.

5. Augustine, *On the Trinity,* preamble 6.1.22: see also, e.g., 1.2.4 (*NPNF*$^1$ 3:19).

6. "Now is the judgment of this world; now the ruler of this world will be driven out." John 12:31.

## Chapter 5

1. Veli-Matti Kärkkäinen, *The Holy Spirit: A Guide to Christian Theology* (Louisville, KY: Westminster John Knox Press, 2012), 29

2. But sometimes a mediator was needed in order to translate one's spiritual experiences into words or pictures, as in the case of the pictures drawn based on Hildegard of Bingen's descriptions. Similarly, great artists often captured the moment better than those who experienced it, as in the case of Bernini's famous statue, the *Ecstasy of Saint Teresa.*

3. Diana Eck, *Encountering God: A Spiritual Journey from Bozeman to Banaras* (Boston: Beacon, 2003), 122, 128.

4. Pope Francis's request for "good vibrations" was reported in Philip Pullella, "Pope Francis 'Prayer' Request to Journalists: 'Send Me Good Vibrations,'" *Huffington Post*, June 8, 2015, https://tinyurl.com/y92zqz68.

5. "Attorney: Woman Thought God Told Her to Kill Sons," CNN, March 30, 2004, https://tinyurl.com/y73wxw76.

6. John Calvin, *Institutes of the Christian Religion,* trans. Henry Beveridge (Peabody: Hendrickson, 2008), 1.7.4, p. 32.

7. Calvin, *Institutes* 1.8.13.

8. Calvin, *Institutes* 3.1.4.

9. John Calvin, *Commentary on Ephesians* (Waikato, New Zealand: Titus Books, 2013), 1:14.

## Chapter 6

1. The word *pneumatology*, meaning the study of the nature of the Holy Spirit, comes from the Greek πνεῦμα, or *pneuma*, meaning breath. In the influential Stoic philosophy, the word meant the "breath of life." Ancient Greek medicine placed human *pneuma* in the sperm and gave the female no credit for what becomes the human born of intercourse, other than being a receptacle to grow the male seed and *pneuma*.

2. Kimberly Hutchings, *Hegel and Feminist Philosophy* (Cambridge: Polity, 2003), 8.

3. Just as Nietzsche's works were used to cast him as an anti-Semite, it is easy to stumble on some of his thoughts about women

and ignore his deeper conceptions of the lives of men and women being controlled by convention and roles, rather than by innate faculties.

4. Elizabeth A. Johnson, *She Who Is: The Mystery of God in Feminine Theological Discourse* (New York: Crossroads, 1993), 83.

5. Johnson, *She Who Is*, 83.

6. For more discussion, read Johnson, *She Who Is*.

7. Johnson, *She Who Is*, 85.

8. Johnson, *She Who Is*, 86.

9. Johnson, *She Who Is*, 86.

10. "Inter-Orthodox Consultation after the Canberra Assembly," World Council of Churches, September 16, 1991, https://tinyurl.com/y9h93nqx.

11. See Grace Ji-Sun Kim, *The Grace of Sophia: A Korean North American Women's Christology* (Cleveland: Pilgrim, 2002).

## Chapter 7

1. Kirsteen Kim, *The Holy Spirit in the World: A Global Conversation* (Maryknoll, NY: Orbis, 2007), 33, 34.

2. Karl Barth, *Church Dogmatics: The Doctrine of Reconciliation,* Vol. 4, Pt.1, trans. G. W. Bromiley (Edinburgh: Bloomsbury T&T Clark, 2004), 645.

3. Mark Oppenheimer, "A Death Row Inmate Finds Common Ground with Theologians," *New York Times*, February 27, 2015, https://tinyurl.com/ybeq9ss3.

4. John B. Cobb Jr., "The Holy Spirit and the Present Age," in *The Lord and Giver of Life: Perspectives on Constructive Pneumatology*, ed. David H. Jensen (Louisville: Westminster John Knox, 2008), 149.

5. Peter C. Hodgson, *Christian Faith: A Brief Introduction* (Louisville: Westminster John Knox, 2001), 140.

6. Sallie McFague, "'The Dearest Freshness Deep Down Things': Some Reflections on the Holy Spirit and Climate Change," in *The Lord and Giver of Life: Perspectives on Constructive Pneumatology*, ed. David H. Jensen (Louisville: Westminster John Knox, 2008), 117.

7. Ken Cohen, *The Way of Qigong* (New York: Wellspring/Ballantine, 1999), 23.

8. There are similar imageries of Isis and Sophia in biblical passages such as Proverbs 8:22ff and Proverbs 1:22ff. For more

discussion please read Grace Ji-Sun Kim, *The Grace of Sophia: A Korean North American Women's Christology* (Cleveland: Pilgrim, 2002).

9. For more discussion of Christianity moving to the Global South, read Philip Jenkins, *The New Faces of Christianity* (Oxford: Oxford University Press, 2008).

10. For more discussion of the similarities between Isis and Hokmah, see Kim, *The Grace of Sophia*.

## Chapter 8

1. Jung Young Lee, *The Trinity in Asian Perspective* (Nashville: Abingdon, 1996), 97.

2. Hans Küng and Julia Ching, *Christianity and Chinese Religions* (London: SCM, 1993), 266.

3. *The Complete Works of Zhuangzi*, trans. Burton Watson (New York: Columbia University Press, 2013), 50.

4. Küng and Ching, *Christianity and Chinese Religions*, 2.

5. A tame example of such an unjust system is a political faction that gains power and then revises voting rules to increase its chances of sustaining its advantages from voting. Gerrymandering and voter qualification rules are two such measures.

## Acknowledgments

1. Augustine, *On the Spirit and the Letter* 5 (*NPNF*[1] 5:84).